FOR SYLVIA

FOR SYLVIA

An Honest Account

VALENTINE ACKLAND

Foreword by Bea Howe

METHUEN

A METHUEN PAPERBACK

First published in 1985 by
Chatto & Windus: The Hogarth Press
This paperback edition published in 1986
by Methuen London Ltd
11 New Fetter Lane, London EC4P 4EE

Reproduced, printed and bound in Great Britain by
Hazell Watson & Viney Limited,
Member of the BPCC Group,
Aylesbury, Bucks

ISBN 0 413 60610 4

Foreword

FOREWORD *by Bea Howe*

It was a raw winter's day in January 1931 with the afternoon light beginning to fail when I got out of the London train at Wool station to see Sylvia hurrying towards me. We met and kissed one another.

'How lovely to see you, darling. You've made it at last,' she said, adding, 'Valentine is waiting in the car outside.'

We proceeded along the narrow wooden platform with Sylvia talking non-stop. There was so much to say, to ask and reply to, for we had not seen each other since my wedding just a year before. I had been abroad for six months on a protracted honeymoon and then busy setting up house in a quiet Kensington cul-de-sac.

In the meantime, Sylvia had left London for Dorset where she had bought a cottage at Chaldon Herring which lay in a green valley winding down to the sea, known to us both since 1920. She was living with a young woman called Valentine Ackland, aged twenty-four, of whom I knew nothing except what Sylvia had informed me in a letter. An unhappy marriage at nineteen, annulled; before, a lonely and at times emotionally disturbed childhood and adolescence. That was all. 'But I do want you two to meet,' she added. And so here I was, but unfortunately only for the night. A flying visit.

There were a number of cars waiting in the station yard where once there had been a few wagonettes and farm carts. We reached Valentine seated at the wheel of a small, green car. It was pretty dusky by now and all I saw was a tall girl, bare-headed, with hair cut very short, wearing trousers, scarf and jacket. She smiled, a faint hesitant smile, as she opened her door and I got in, while Sylvia, still talking, occupied the back seat.

It was quite dark when we drew up before the late Miss Green's cottage, small, slate-roofed, which Sylvia had acquired because it was totally unpicturesque, stood by itself and had a garden with possibilities.

Tea followed and Valentine disappeared as Sylvia and I sat on either side of a log fire deep in conversation till sherry time.

An evening meal came next, delicious, and after coffee Valentine left us. On and on we talked till, suddenly, I felt we were not alone. Another was present. Glancing up, I saw Valentine, who had changed into a silk shirt and Morocco slippers and was standing in the shadowy archway of the door opening into a passage. She stood there, silent but watchful. The theatrical image of someone waiting in the wings to make an entrance on stage flashed before me. But when? At what precise moment? Evidently not then. For even as I looked that shadowy figure vanished, and it was to be many years before Valentine finally emerged from the wings of Sylvia's private life to take any part in mine. However Valentine *did* reappear later, that evening, to drive me to Mrs Way, with whom I was lodged for the night.

The following day was icy cold but fine, with a brilliant light. A picnic lunch packed, we set out for Lulworth to revive old memories, said Sylvia. It was from The Weld Arms, East Lulworth – where Sylvia, Stephen Tomlin, my brother and I had spent Easter of 1920 – that Tommy, as everyone called him, had disappeared on a walking tour to discover Chaldon Herring, while we returned to London.

Seated beside Valentine, an expert driver, with Sylvia and William, her black chow, behind, I glanced now and then at her profile. It was a handsome head, the impassive face pale, and the full eyes, slightly hooded, a bluish-grey. When they did turn on me after I had made a casual remark, they were sad eyes. They did not light up. I was intrigued by Valentine's immaculate appearance. Although she was wearing a skirt (not trousers) her coat was masculine in style and her driving-gloves and shoes expensive-looking. Gloves and shoes made of the best leather were essential to Valentine, as were her purses, hand-bags and, in later life, her spectacle-cases. I know because I inherited some. Anything made of nylon or plastic was abhorrent to her. In an odd way, Valentine's dressing of herself was a kind of protective clothing such as Nature gives to disguise an animal living in the wild. That Valentine was shy, almost painfully so, I had already discovered before Sylvia informed me of this during our after-supper talk.

Our excursion to Lulworth was a happy one and at five o'clock we reached Wareham, where I was to catch the train back to London. Sylvia saw me off, and when my train was signalled we made a hasty plan to meet on her next visit to town.

'I can put you up – and Valentine, too, of course,' I said.

Sylvia laughed, her short-sighted eyes gleaming amused behind her horn-rimmed glasses.

'That will have to wait,' she replied. 'Valentine won't come – but, perhaps, some day!' Then, as my train came to a shuddering halt, 'Oh, damn! Get in, darling. It doesn't wait a minute.' So in I got with Sylvia waving me off.

In a corner seat of an empty compartment I thought over my visit to Sylvia. Nothing had been changed between us by Valentine's arrival in her life. It was the same old relationship, sprung long ago from our first meeting, when we had each recognized quickly a mutual affection, regard and understanding that continued through the years till Sylvia's death. But what more did I know of Valentine since meeting her? Very little. That she was painfully shy, yes, and wrote poetry which, no doubt, Sylvia was encouraging as she had once encouraged me in my writing. Characteristically, Sylvia had made no attempt to draw Valentine into our conversation or to try to make a threesome of my visit. In point of fact, Valentine had been conspicuously absent from our company. Still, I intuitively felt that she had become the most important person in Sylvia's present life. I was glad.

In her thirty-eighth year, fully established as a poet and novelist of distinction and originality, Sylvia, as a young girl, had suffered a tragic loss through the death of her father, George Townsend Warner, Head of the Modern Side of Harrow School and a distinguished teacher and scholar. This loss had been followed by the marriage of her mother, strong-minded, autocratic, to an ex-pupil of her husband, much nearer in age to Sylvia than herself: on her leaving Harrow for Devon, Sylvia now twenty-three, departed to earn her own living in London. This she did by joining the editorial board of the Church Music Project, that was being sponsored by the Carnegie Trust. During this very influential period of her life, which resulted in her becoming an authority on Tudor music, she became involved in a relationship which helped her not only to overcome the loss of her father but to end her personal loneliness. There was no question of marriage on either side, and after some years it finished as discreetly as it had begun with Sylvia restored emotionally, a mature, completely 'rounded-off' woman. The immediately successful publication of her first novel *Lolly Willowes* (1926) assured her of a literary career should she wish to pursue one in preference to remaining in the world of musicology. She chose the former alternative.

Unfortunately there followed another affair for Sylvia, very different from her first one. It was with a young man, her junior, who had been at Harrow. Charmer though he was, and Sylvia's equal in intellect and wit, he was emotionally unbalanced, and took from Sylvia's generosity far more than he was prepared to give in return. His eventual departure affected her deeply, wounding her pride and creating a wide gap in her life.

But now, sitting in my train as it rushed through darkness to London, I felt that the tall, silent girl I had met was going to fill, perhaps, that gap. Sylvia had a strong maternal streak in her compassionate and essentially *caring* character. She always needed someone to cherish and protect.

I did not see Valentine again till the summer of 1933, when I went to stay with Sylvia in a lovely old seventeenth-century house, Frankfort Manor in Norfolk, which had been rented with the hope that it might become a future home. Valentine's mother, a widow, did not live so far off – at Winterton, on the coast – so on the day following my arrival we went by car to visit her. The Hill, where Valentine had spent much of her early life, had, so far as I can remember, little to distinguish it from any seaside villa or holiday home of the Edwardian period. Beyond the garden with its tall trees which Valentine had climbed when young, retiring for hours into their branches with a small chess set and a wooden board on which she composed poems or penned numerous letters to

11

imaginary people, lay a remote stretch of sand dunes covered with marram grass, softly blowing that afternoon. Seeing my pleasure in this landscape of sand, sea and wide open East Anglian sky, she suggested that we might go down to the shore. So down we went, leaving Sylvia to cope with a loquacious Mrs Ackland.

As we clambered over the dunes, Valentine began to talk to me more easily than she had before, pointing out Winterton Ness, the most easterly point in England. This was her home ground, I realized, where as a child she had played, bird-watched and been her happiest. She has described this time in an autobiographical poem as her

Light days; the beautiful solitude of trees,
Green leaves a refuge, smooth branches to fondle;
The dandling sea nursed me, the sand was soft and gentle.
Larks sang and I was unwatched for long hours of clear daylight.

The following day we drove to East Dereham where John Craske and his wife, Laura, lived. An ex-Winterton fisherman, John Craske had been paralyzed as the result of being blown up in his ship while at sea during the First World War. He was a discovery of Valentine's who, on taking him a bowl of soup one day in his cottage, found him surrounded by paintings done on any kind of material to hand, such as cardboard, paper and even a piece of wood. Others were skilfully embroidered with bright wools on canvas or on one of his wife's pudding cloths.

Impressed by his talent, best described as belonging to the Douanier Rousseau or Grandma Moses school of primitive painters, Valentine bought some. Later, after seeing these pictures in Valentine's London flat, Dorothy

12

Warren organized an exhibition for Craske in her Gallery, with immediate success.

The rest of my stay at Frankfort passed quietly, with Valentine disappearing at intervals, in particular to her room in the evening. But one souvenir remains with me of Frankfort: a snapshot taken by Valentine of Sylvia and myself as we sat, unaware, deep in conversation, one on each side of the handsome Georgian fireplace.

It was at Frankfort that poor failing William was put to sleep and his grave dug by Valentine. Sylvia never owned another dog. From now on she gave her heart to cats; cats tame or wild needing a home, and above all to a beloved succession of Siamese who were always in total possession of the house. Unfortunately Frankfort Manor was found too expensive to be considered as a permanent home and sadly, with a newly acquired cat and a goat, Victoria Ambrosia, they moved back to Chaldon.

In the mid-Thirties, life became very hectic for Sylvia and me. My husband's career at the BBC took off in a big way and I was much involved, while Sylvia was caught up in a new world: that of politics. She joined, temporarily, the Communist party in sympathy to what was going on in Spain and Nazi Germany. In September 1937, Valentine and she left Chaldon for Spain to give assistance for three weeks at the Red Cross Bureau in Barcelona. Some months later, they decided to leave Chaldon and acquire larger premises than a cottage. They found a suitable house, Frome Vauchurch, a short walk out of Maiden Newton, but as final arrangements were taking place they were off once more, in June 1938, on a writers' delegation to the Congress of the International Association in Defence of Culture that was being held in Madrid and Valencia.

After their return, they moved to Frome Vauchurch, which they came to like more and more and where they both died – Valentine on 9 November 1969 and Sylvia on 1 May 1978.

Frome Vauchurch was a curious tall box of a house devoid of any architectural feature. It stood beside the river Frome, only separated from it on one side by a narrow plank path complete with a handrail. Walking along it was reminiscent of being on a ship's deck. To Valentine's delight, the river was full of trout and she became an ardent piscator, buying herself a strange silvered object known as a 'priest' with which one gave the final quietus to a landed but still struggling trout.

When I first saw Frome Vauchurch, I fell instantly for its peculiar charm. It was the close proximity of the river bubbling and rippling so sweetly along past the house that created a unique atmosphere, as well as its being the haunt of moorhens, voles and swans. I have always been attracted to the beauty of swans, and Valentine shared this love with me. In the years to come she often sent me a snapshot of the Frome swans and I replied with a cutting from some magazine or a poem relating to these beautiful birds.

Soon the possibility of a European war began to overshadow our lives. In April 1939, Sylvia made tentative plans to obtain visas to attend the third American Writers' Conference that was being organized in New York to consider the loss of democracy in Europe. When these visas were granted, Sylvia and Valentine left England with a rich female American friend in tow.

By June, Sylvia was sharing a house in Connecticut for six weeks with, as she put humorously in a letter, 'two petticoats (both in trousers)'! But when war broke out between England and Germany in September, Sylvia was back in New York, informing William Maxwell, a fiction editor of the *New Yorker*, that in spite of pressure from her American friends and fans to stay, she was returning to her homeland. 'I have the profoundest doubts of this war,' she wrote, 'and I suppose that going back will not better it for me. But for all that I feel my responsibilities are there not here.'

It was the right decision and Valentine went with her, interrupting a disastrous liaison which had begun between the American friend and herself.

Luckily for us, my husband's Department at the BBC had been evacuated to Evesham on the outbreak of war, so I was able with the aid of my bicycle and a fascinating cross-country journey taken by little trains to see Sylvia at Frome Vauchurch from time to time. But I saw nothing of Valentine, as she was out all day working for a doctor in his dispensary.

When the war ended Mark and I went on a long-promised visit to Sylvia. He had not yet met Valentine and I was slightly apprehensive, but there was no need: they liked one another from the first, sharing a common interest in astrology besides collecting period playing-cards, and Tarot ones in particular.

It must have been at about this time that Valentine approached a major crisis in her life. For nineteen years, unknown to Sylvia and others, she had been a 'secret drinker'. Over the years she had sought medical advice to cure herself of this habit but had received little help. She had first become addicted to drink to overcome her painful shyness as a young girl when meeting people and attending social functions.

However on the evening of 8 October 1947, before

stumbling into bed after a secret session, she fell on her knees at Frome Vauchurch in total misery and despair. What religious belief, what faith, she had once had as an Anglo-Catholic child, then as a nineteen-year-old girl wishing to enter the Catholic Church before marriage, was dead. In the appalling emptiness of space and swirling darkness she felt surrounding her at that moment, she cried: 'Is God there?' Though no answer came back, she vowed then and there, without hope or reason, that she would stop drinking.

She woke next morning feeling weak and ill, but managed to carry on through the day. When evening came, she found herself to her astonishment 'walking in tranquillity', as she described it. Moreover this feeling persisted with another of complete assurance that she would conquer her drinking problem, which she did in time. But this 'spiritual crisis' was followed by another, which was to affect not only her life but Sylvia's as well. It was prompted by the approaching visit to Frome Vauchurch of the American friend who had already caused trouble, and with whom Valentine confessed to Sylvia she was in love. Furthermore, she declared that she could *truly* love two people at the same time; two people who were poles apart, and this knowledge was tearing her in half. Valentine appears to have always been aware of a division in herself, a dual nature, as this autobiographical poem shows:

Since childhood choice has always been my worst besetter;
Which of two colours? Which of two odours? Which of two favours?
Which of two saviours?
Should I grow up promotor or begetter? Should I leap the barricades
Shout 'Liberty!' and die, Or live obscurely, in humility,

and scale the highest heights none but the blind can see,
The blind who have met their Lord and been restored to see.

The result of much painful discussion with Valentine led Sylvia, now in her fifty-sixth year, to write to an old friend, Alyse Gregory, the widow of Llewelyn Powys, who was living at Chydyock, West Chaldon:

5:VI:1949

... So in a month or a couple of months Valentine and —— will be living together. Here, in this house, I hope. It seems much the best plan. It will assure Valentine a continuity of work and trees growing and books, some of her roots will remain in the same ground. It will settle —— with a certain degree of responsible domesticity, which will be much more settling to her nerves than flitting from hotel to hotel; and for my part, I would rather have the sting than the muffle of staying. Practically, too, it is much easier to find a roof for one than for two ...

But the main reason why I am telling you this is that for the first time I have been able to feel a living and in-my-flesh belief that Valentine may one day return to me. Till now I have assented to this belief with something more calculating than hope and more tremulous than reason; and chiefly because I love her cannot bear to disbelieve her assurances. But yesterday, I saw her not only more shaken by the news in the cable than I (that could be accounted for by her doubled state of mind) but – what is the word – the word is very nearly *appalled*. It seemed to me as though this was the first time she had realized herself as living without me, that, until now, solicitude had always presented it to her as *me living without her* ... It was not for long ... But it was there and I saw it. Even if I never see it, again ... I cannot tell if it will make the immediate future easier ... But it was there and I saw it and so I want to tell you.*

*from *The Letters of Sylvia Townsend Warner* edited by William Maxwell (Chatto & Windus and The Viking Press, 1982).

Out of her love and understanding of Valentine it was Sylvia who finally made the supreme sacrifice of leaving Frome Vauchurch, *her* home for nineteen years. She was also leaving *her* cats, *her* books and the garden she had made. However, through this selfless act the scales of Valentine's ultimate decision were tipped towards her and not towards the one coming over the water to Dorset.

Before that arrival Valentine went on agonizing till she could bear it no longer and sat down to write in soul-searching honesty, sparing herself nothing, a record of everything that had happened to her in childhood, in adolescence and as a young woman. She finished this account on the 4th of July and gave it to Sylvia.

For those who now read this document, it must be remembered that Valentine was a child of her own time. A child born of conventional, well-off parents, who gave her the expensive but, on the whole, poor education then fashionable. Neither Valentine's education nor her parents, whose views were so alien to her own, were of any help in the strange situations she found herself placed, largely through ignorance.

Lesbianism. Homosexuality. These were words unknown to Valentine and to other girls of her class background. In the 1920s London's social world was a strange one to enter, for a vacuum had been created by the War, causing the break-down of old conventions and codes of moral behaviour which had not yet been replaced by others of a more liberal nature.

At this moment of writing, an illuminating article has appeared in *The Times* entitled 'My Lesbian Daughter'. It tells the story of how one still conservative mother reacted when informed by her daughter that she was 'gay'. After much argument and discussion mother and daughter

18

came to have a much closer and more loving relationship than before this revelation occurred. Such an open conversation could never have taken place between Valentine and her parents (one a West End London dentist, hide-bound and intolerant, the other an emotional High Anglo-Catholic), any more than the moving account of her life, 'for Sylvia', could be written by a girl of today.

By September Sylvia had left Frome Vauchurch. I learnt this from a letter dated the 6th of September telling me she was staying at a 'funny' hotel on the outskirts of Yeovil. 'I have basely deserted Valentine though it is by mutual agreement,' she wrote. 'She has an American friend staying with her, not an affliction, for she likes her; but so do not I, said the cookmaid.'

She continued by telling me how she was

Wallowing in walks on Sedgemoor, I take a little train, I take a little bus, and cast myself in those willowy-green, sweet-scented solitudes. Particularly sweet-scented just now for they are gathering the osiers and gently simmering them to get the bark off, and the smell of the simmering is one of the most exquisite smells I have ever known, fine and aromatic and slightly bitter, and infinitely gentle. A true willowy soul.

I knew that Sylvia was very fond of this part of Somerset. It had special memories for her, belonging to the time she visited Wells to work on the Cathedral archives. Putting two and two together I realized things were not well at Frome Vauchurch, the more so when I received a parcel from Sylvia containing a pretty blue-and-white American china money-box in the shape of a bee-hive which she wished to be relieved of. It was an unsolicited gift 'that might be useful as an illustration for one of your articles, darling,' she had added. I did have it photographed but never took to it and it ended up on a bazaar stall.

19

By October, Sylvia was back at Frome Vauchurch and all was well again. Valentine's 'implacable regard for truth' (Sylvia's words) had saved her. She knew now, irrevocably, that she could not live without Sylvia, who had promised her on the first Christmas Day they spent together at Chaldon in 1930 'to stand by her always'. This was the love and sense of security that Valentine had always craved. They each had something to give the other, I think, which they alone could give, and isn't this the base, the keystone, for all enduring human relationships?

In 1950, after a holiday spent in France, they decided to let Frome Vauchurch and spend the winter in Norfolk renting Great Eye Folly, Salthouse, Holt where I paid them a visit from our Essex cottage. It was a folly indeed, standing on a low wind-bitten cliff; in front lay a long pebbly beach on which the cold grey North Sea battered and crashed or, in more benign mood, splashed noisily while gulls screamed overhead. Behind was a cattle marsh and a rough track leading to Salthouse.

Valentine was in her element here. She gathered driftwood on the shore, cleaved a frozen fish for Sylvia to cook, and bird-watched. Sylvia thought it was a brilliant idea to be away from Frome Vauchurch and to have Christmas in this desolate spot. Unfortunately abnormal tides became the order of the day and on one occasion Valentine's own car was almost washed away. They had to pack up and return to Frome Vauchurch in the New Year. Sylvia was sad, for she had found the people of Salthouse and Holt – the baker, the butcher, the grocer etc. – so kind and friendly when shopping there. Now she must leave them to become – as she said – 'the peculiar Miss Warner' in Dorset.

In 1952, Valentine opened a shop at Frome Vauchurch

to sell antiques. For some time she had been attending local auction sales, returning home with all kinds of loot picked up for very little in those days. Victorian china and brass objects, prints, vases, and small pieces of furniture were now crowding what space was available in the house. To hand there was a long, studio-like room clamped on to the east wall of the house which had a door opening on to the gravel drive outside. Empty except for a piano and books, Valentine took over this room for her shop. As soon as the news spread that Miss Ackland was selling antiques, would-be buyers began to appear from near and far, so much so that a bell was bought and attached to the shop door. According to Sylvia, Valentine had 'a pointer's nose' for acquiring objects that would sell. Apart from this flair, Valentine turned out to be a shrewd business woman besides an honest one, asking for only a small margin of profit on what she sold. But her great asset over most antique shop owners I have known was a genuine desire to obtain the exact object one was searching for, whether a colour print, papier mâché tray or Spode teapot. In this way Valentine's help was particularly invaluable to me, as I had become a regular contributor to *The Times* and *Country Life* on nineteenth-century subjects. When I went to Frome Vauchurch I often accompanied her now on a foray to a remote village or market town where she had located something which she thought might do as an illustration to one of my articles. Between us, there always sat in the car a small black poodle – first Fidèle, then Fougère – beloved of Valentine but, though tolerated by Sylvia, not popular additions to the household because of their yapping habits. Valentine was often amused by my taste on these antique trips of ours, but it was an affectionate amusement. So our own relationship was formed.

In the 1950s a change came about from the days when Valentine used to disappear for hours to her room after supper. Now the three of us would retire to *her* sitting-room upstairs. On one visit she taught me how to type, and was a kind and patient teacher. Frome Vauchurch was a far more comfortable house to stay in these days. Night storage heaters were installed and rooms close-carpeted. Sylvia's casual dressing of herself with her mind elsewhere improved under Valentine's vigilant eye, and she came to enjoy acquiring a new outfit.

When Sylvia undertook the translation of Proust's *Contre Sainte-Beuve*, for Chatto & Windus in 1954, she became completely wrapped up in work which was new to her and which made her, as she said, 'very very happy'.

By now Valentine was leading quite a life of her own, her shop having brought her into contact with people who did not actually belong to Sylvia's literary world. The success of Valentine's shop had a stabilizing effect on her. It made her less shy when meeting people. In fact, she acquired some new friends from among her customers. But there remained one side of her complex character untouched by social or material gain, even by her continuing sense of personal security achieved from living at Frome Vauchurch with Sylvia. Deep-rooted in Valentine was a 'spiritual' need never really lost through her emotionally disturbed life from childhood to maturity. This need surfaced, demanding instant attention.

Valentine had realized that above all things, including even her love for Sylvia, she must regain her faith and become a good working Catholic once more. In her own words, 'She needed the support in the careful routine of living, again, as a Catholic.' Once she had achieved this, might she not become the 'whole' and not the 'divided' person she always felt herself to be?

For advice and help she wrote to the London Catholic Centre in March 1955 and was put in touch with Father Gay, an enlightened and kindly priest. In a letter to him, Valentine made a full confession in regard to her broken religious past, and told him how she wished to become a practising Catholic as she had never given up her belief in God. Father Gay's answer was that she must seek a local priest, and make confession to him, when she would receive absolution followed by Holy Communion.

However, at fifty-three Valentine was not the ardent nineteen-year-old girl who had first been converted to Roman Catholicism. The process laid down by Father Gay presented several problems to the adult Valentine. Firstly, there was her 'implacable regard for truth', which now questioned certain tenets held by the Catholic Church on investigation. She could not truthfully believe in some of them. Secondly, though she could go into the confessional box with a clear conscience, how could she take the Holy Sacrament beset with some of her still conflicting doubts and fears?

At this point, to make matters more difficult for her, Sylvia emerged from her long hibernation with Proust to find, much to her distress, that Valentine was contemplating a return to the Catholic church. She wrote off to Paul Nordoff, an American composer with whom she corresponded intimately, telling him that she simply could not understand how Valentine with her particularly honest, constantly analysing brand of mind could possibly consider becoming involved again with such 'an extraordinary mingle-mangle of pettifogging ordinances and assumptions ... ideas I mean, like the sacraments and a priest caste dispensing or witholding a deity in a wafer.'

Sylvia was unhappy because she felt that during her absorption with *Contre Sainte-Beuve* she had failed Valentine, who must have been undergoing both mental and emotional stress to undertake her proposed step. Although Valentine tried to reassure Sylvia that this was not the case and that she had long been thinking of becoming a Catholic again, the situation did not improve between them. In fact, they found it increasingly difficult to talk about religion at all, so that it became almost a taboo subject.

Undeterred, Valentine pursued her solitary way back to the Catholic church. In 1961, her mother died and The Hill was sold. Only one of what Sylvia called 'Valentine's vampire relations' remained, her widowed sister, Joan, who had so bullied and persecuted her as a child. Forgetting the past, Valentine generously took her on, listening to her complaints and writing to her almost daily.

In October 1963, with Valentine in poor health owing to a thyroid condition, they went to Italy, on what was to be their last and happiest expedition abroad.

Early in 1964, Sylvia was approached to write the biography of T. H. White. She accepted the commission and soon became as involved with White as she had been with Proust.

Having suffered a prolonged, non-creative period caused by emotional and religious problems, Valentine was also busy writing, faithful to a lifelong ambition to capture and transfix the true character of the elusive, fleeting moment, whether she stood, alone, observing the flight of swans over the Frome or sitting in what was to her the always safe security of a leafy wood, fighting despair.

Such poems which try to convey what Virginia Woolf so exquisitely expressed in her essay 'The Moment' were published in 1973 – their title *The Nature of the Moment*. But other poems of a different genre which she called her 'private' poems are all deeply religious. Only one, 'Night Prayer', appeared in the *Tablet* in December 1968:

> From strict confinement of line, the harsh
> Cords of time constriction, from rhyme
> And exactitude and all that prisons the wind –
> Libera me, Domine.

> From all that snares and baffles, that tear, from the marsh
> Gases, polluted air, false clues, craven fear
> And the long preliminaries leading no-where –
> Libera me, Domine.

> Libera me: breathe on this heavy clay
> The word it would say, waiting and waiting till it may
> Breathe at last – Glorificamus Te
> Domine.

In March 1968 Valentine had to see her doctor owing to the pain in her left breast. Cancer was diagnosed and she entered the Nuffield Ward of Guy's Hospital, London, where an operation was performed by Sir Hedley Atkins on the 10th of April. It was considered successful, and Valentine and Sylvia returned to Frome Vauchurch. Unfortunately, later on in the year Valentine had to undergo a second operation, which took place on the 19th of December. It was a tiring and unhappy time for Sylvia who stayed at the Goring Hotel, where I saw her.

Early in the New Year they were able to return home and Sylvia, now seventy-five, was determined not to look into the future till she had to! Endeavouring to give

Valentine every support within her power and knowing, too, she had ceased going to Mass, Sylvia accompanied her when she attended Quaker meetings in Dorchester, for Valentine seemed to be obtaining spiritual comfort from them.

During this period Valentine seemed possessed of tireless energy, tearing about the countryside in her car, Fougère seated as always beside her. But this brief interlude of revitalization did not last long. Her left shoulder began to stiffen, and with the increasing pain she found that she could not type or drive her car except with difficulty. Another visit to Sir Hedley Atkins was taken and he located the spread of cancer to her lungs. A course of hormone pills followed to contain the disease, but they only brought extreme fatigue, depression and sickness.

Scrupulously honest as ever, and possibly because she wished to make a last confession to Father Gay, Valentine wrote to him on the 18th of July. She had had to stop going to Mass, she told him, and taking Holy Communion, because she no longer believed that there was one *true* Church, only one in its *widest* sense. She was also troubled not from lack of faith in the Blessed Trinity or the Gospels, but because she simply could not stand up in church and repeat the whole Creed in complete honesty. Valentine concluded her last letter to Father Gay stressing her still unshakeable faith in the power of prayer adding, 'even now I hope you will pray forgivingly for me. VALENTINE.'

It was the old, old story, that was never to find a satisfactory solution for her in this world. By October there was no question but that she was very ill. Cancer had spread rapidly. Only one consolation remained: she and Sylvia were *together*, in every sense of that comforting word. Doctor Hollins told Sylvia that he had no intention of removing Valentine to a hospital in Dorchester. She could be nursed at home. And so she was, and Sylvia managed.

In her room, Valentine lay listening to the familiar sounds, long loved, of the river she had wandered by and fished. Though her binoculars were put away like her rod, the broad clear square of her bedroom window was left for her to watch – as she did – the flight of birds that crossed it diagonally from dawn to sunset. It inspired a poem of hers, one of the last, that later Sylvia had printed and made into a New Year card, which she sent to me in 1974. In her poem, Valentine describes the steady sombre passage of rooks, outward and homeward-bound; the pigeons' hasty passing; the lovely dart and dive of seagulls over the Frome; but best of all

> ... in chequered and patterned cover,
> Shaken out, drawn back, folded, spread again over
> All my window of sky, there fly the plover.

An impassioned lover of life which, in so many tortuous ways, she had lived, up to the hilt, Valentine had no wish to die. She was only sixty-three. But there is no short cut to death for a cancer victim; no instantaneous finish such as that which follows a massive cerebral stroke or the plunging down from sky to earth like Icarus in an airline disaster. Though inevitable, cancer's end is slow till merciful drugs take over. There is no doubt that her illness struck Valentine a cruel blow, for she had believed in ultimate recovery. But stoically, methodically and with care, in the way she had typed and sent out her catalogues to her regular customers, Valentine made lists of bequests

27

and what she wanted done, choosing the words to mark her gravestone (she is buried in the little churchyard at Chaldon Herring): NON OMNIS MORIAR – 'Death is not the end.'

By now Fougère was considered too heavy to lie on her bed and his place was taken by a tiny silvery-grey soft and cuddly kitten named Moth.

I knew nothing of what was happening at Frome Vauchurch since a September letter from Sylvia. For she knew that I was experiencing a traumatic time myself, having decided to sell our Essex house where we had been living for the last five years and to return to London. We made our move at the beginning of November, and on entering our garden flat there on the doormat was a letter from Sylvia wishing us good fortune and happiness in our new home. A few days later came another telling me Valentine had died on the morning of Sunday the 9th of November. Before she had been put under morphia, they had discussed whether I should be told of Valentine's approaching death, but they had decided against it. Typically, Sylvia did not wish 'to cross your new threshold with news that Valentine was mortally ill,' she wrote.

I went to Frome Vauchurch as soon as I could. For the first time in many years there was no Sylvia to greet me on the platform of Dorchester station; nor was Valentine waiting in her car outside. I was met by Mr King, a kindly man, who kept the garage at Maiden Newton. I discovered that Fougère now lived with him and his wife. As we drove up the short gravel drive which stopped outside the doors of Valentine's closed shop, I saw Sylvia waiting for me on the small verandah of the house. The front door was open behind her. We kissed and went in.

'Before we settle down, I want to show you something,' she said, and led the way upstairs.

The house seemed peculiarly empty and quiet. There was no Fougère, I realized, to bark one a welcome. We reached Sylvia's bedroom and entered. Immediately I saw what it was she wanted to show me. There, on the wall above the fireplace and directly opposite her bed, hung a portrait. A drawing, most delicately, beautifully drawn, showing Valentine's pillowed head with eyes closed as if asleep rather than in the final stillness of death.

'Oh, Sylvia! How peaceful she looks,' I said.

'Yes,' she replied, 'I think I told you in my letter how death renewed her. Youth came flooding back into her careworn face. I rang up Joy Finzi to come over. She did, and drew her.'

We stood together in silence with pale winter sunshine lighting the room. Then we went downstairs.

Was it two or three years later, I cannot remember, when I received from Sylvia a small paper-bound booklet entitled: *Later Poems* by Valentine Ackland 1906–1969. Opening it I saw the poem on its first page and read it. Instantly, I was back at Frome Vauchurch on a winter afternoon, with Sylvia standing beside me as we looked in silence at Valentine's pillowed head in that portrait hanging on the wall in her bedroom.

> When you look at me, after I have died,
> And note the tidy hair, the sleeping head,
> Closed eyes and quiet hands – Do not decide
> Too readily that I was so. Instead,
> Look at your own heart while you may and see
> How wild and strange a live man is, and so remember me.

For Sylvia: an Honest Account

FOR SYLVIA

One I loved so dearly

Because I tended long,

And by her death I ambushed

Alone the wild black swan.

from 'Sleep', 26 June 1968

Frome Vauchurch 4 July 1949

My Love,

I have finished this tonight, as best I can; and it is for you. It is strange to think that probably this is all I have given you, this record of blundering from shame to shame, with so much glory shining down on me all the time, and most brightly from you, who are my sun.

I forgot to put in the secular quotation which stands best for us, and has been sword and shield to me ever since you wrote it down in pencil on the flyleaf of the book you gave me for Christmas, 1930: 'Never heed,' said the girl, 'I'll stand by you.' I'm a coward, my Love, and I have heeded far too often, but that has made no difference to the truth of this that you wrote down for me: let it be true to our lives' end, Sylvia –

Valentine – who loves you.

[1]

In an honest account of a life two things are necessary and another desirable: first, anonymity, so that the author may be honest, if he can; although anonymity will probably disgruntle the reader, who likes to feel sure that he would at once recognize an author – especially an author of 'confessions' – if he met him; and likes to know for certain that it is possible to meet him. In order, therefore, that the reader shall not give way to an impulse to return the book unread to the lending library the second thing is necessary: that the 'crisis' of the life shall be presented as quickly as possible, before the reader's boredom has set in. The 'crisis' is not necessarily the most exciting event in a life, nor is it often the most emotional or even the most interesting to read about; but it is certainly the most stimulating, to author and reader alike, and besides, it has the quality of a winnowing wind which powerfully and for ever separates the husk from the grain and blows away all readers who, from difference of nature or from immaturity, are inimical to ripeness. The third, the desirable thing in a book of this kind, is variety, and that is really a matter of presentation on the author's part and perception on the reader's. All lives without exception are of infinite variety, but not all owners of lives have inclinations to study the eccentricities of pattern, and not all readers have eyesight acute enough to trace the pattern even when it is pointed out.

Anonymity is fairly easy to assume, even in a Modern

State. Fill in a typical Government Form, for instance, leaving blanks for the Christian Names(s) Surname and National Registration Number. Thus: *Sex*: F. *Age*: 42. *Nationality*: British. *Height*: 5 ft. 11 inches. *Colour of Hair*: Brown. *Colour of Eyes*: Grey. *Special Peculiarities*: None. *Place of Birth*: London. *Married or Single*: ... Here, though the answer would not endanger anonymity, we stop. The answer to this question, and to any others the Form sets out, will not doubt be supplied in the course of this work.

The 'crisis': it has been laid down that this should grip the reader's interest, grapple him to the author, and make it impossible for him to put the book down until he has finished it, or at least impossible for him to return it to the lending library by the next post. But the 'crisis' in this particular life is very difficult to describe; for one thing, it is hard to know whether it happened in a flash or whether, in point of fact, it matured rather slowly and broke, as it were, creamily and in silence. This 'crisis', too, is not directly concerned with a sexual upheaval, which makes it perhaps less enthralling to the reader than it was to the author. However; it happened, and it was undoubtedly the sharpest possible crisis any life can know, for all it was so quiet and did not so much as cause a ripple on the surface of domestic life.

On the night of 8 October 1947 the subject of this book stumbled miserably to bed. For reasons, some of which will appear and some of which are unknown to me, I had become helplessly addicted to drink and for nineteen years, struggling most of the time to free myself, I had been caught in the net. Diaries – even small engagement books – for all those years are marked with the letters 'DD' or 'TMD' (Devoid of Drink and Too Much Drink, respectively).

In about 1928, when I was twenty-two, I had devised this childish code, and thought that if I could mark off day by day the progress made, I might eventually free myself. I would be encouraged, I thought, towards the end of the year to find that 'DD' outnumbered 'TMD.' But it never did.

At this early stage I was not cravenly ashamed of my condition. I was frightened by it, and sharply aware of the danger, but I had two ideas about it. First, I felt that I should not burden with my vice anyone who loved me; it was my private enemy and I should fight it without endangering them. It *would* endanger them, I thought, to be told of it by me; love is so precious to the one who loves, so compassionate and chivalrous and headlong: I thought it would be blasphemous selfishness to look to them for help. That this was a genuine belief, held for the reasons I have given, is proved by the fact that I did not hesitate to call in mercenary troops – or try to. In 1927 I had some small illness and took that chance to tell the doctor that I was already caught up in this habit of drinking; would he help me? I remember that I spoke very honestly to him, although I suppose with shyness and aware that it was a curious, embarrassing confession to hear from a young woman of twenty-one, well-dressed and apparently already situated quite pleasantly in life. He was a Roman Catholic doctor; a saturnine man with a good reputation and a stupid, self-satisfied face. He looked at me with distaste and replied that such a thing was a matter for private attention; he could do nothing for me.

About a year later, when my diary was already proving to me that 'TMD' far outweighed 'DD', I went back to the same doctor and asked very earnestly for help, or for him to suggest where I might find it. But again he looked at me

39

with distaste and answered that nothing whatever could be done, and no assistance could be given – much less any sort of cure. 'There is no cure at all,' he said pontifically. 'If you can't help yourself, no one can help you.'

That year, too, I was by chance involved with a very famous physician, a man well-known for his interest in art and women. I did not think that his feeling for me need inhibit me from asking for his help. He often talked to me about the foibles and strange psychological tangles he discovered in his patients; he did not talk kindly, but he showed a certain shrewdness and I thought I must take this chance – I was becoming exhausted by my struggles and evidently I was not able to help myself. It was difficult to ask this man, but I desperately ventured it. I remember that I chose a bad moment; after a good dinner, when we were back in my apartment, when undoubtedly he thought I would go to bed with him, and I had been for some time promisingly silent and – as it must have seemed – shyly apprehensive of what was to come.

It was a bad moment, but I knew my courage would not last, and so I spoke quickly: 'Can you help me?' I said. 'I have got into a desperate state, I think. I can't do without drink. I think about it all day; I can't do anything at all, write or read or meet people, without getting really half-drunk beforehand ... Is there anything you can do to help me stop?'

These are almost exactly the words I said, I am sure. And then he laughed and laughed. His small eyes screwed up in his head, with tears coming out of the corners.

'You!' he said at last, 'Well, my dear child! Now, why worry at all about it? You are very young, you know, and it will soon wear off. Vanity alone will be enough to stop you! When you find yourself getting fat and blowsy, with tearful eyes and shaking hands, you'll soon stop all right! Now – '

In the next year, and the next, I went on. Happy years, in the main; and busy years. Many things happened which are worth recounting later in this book; but although I once more asked for help (each time of course, it was harder, because of the rebuffs, and because as I grew older I became subconsciously much more timid: not trusting now to the charm of youth or the claim youth feels it has on mercy and compassion), the doctor I invoked this time told me that he had conquered this same weakness – easily, he gave me to understand – and that, while he could not help me except by his example, he could assure me that very few people ever did overcome it, and that the prognosis was bad, very bad indeed.

Then, in 1940, I was almost overwhelmed by public and private worries, and although I had scarcely any money I spent £25 on a commercial 'cure' which did let me out, as it were, on parole for about six weeks. But I returned again and was once more trapped and netted. And so lay in misery until 1947.

In that year, in the summer, I made a great effort and for a month was free. Then I fell back again, more hopelessly than ever, and so at last came to that evening of October 8th, when I stumbled into my bedroom, scarcely sensible except of sickness and despair.

As I was about to get into bed I felt, in my reeling head, as if eternity were opening all around me; and it was black as hell.

I had no 'beliefs'. Recently I had been reading the old philosophers, the Stoics particularly, and wondering vaguely enough whether man was irrevocably immortal, or whether he could become immortal; whether he was something or nothing. But I had come to no conclusions and I was not in a state to think.

On that strange night, however, for no reason that I can give, instead of climbing into bed and putting out the light (which was the only thing I wanted to do) I knelt down and – with this vertiginous black Eternity surrounding me – addressed Emptiness like this: 'Is God there?'

There was no reply. Everything was completely dead. I had no sense except of emptiness and the rushing swirling dark.

'Very well,' I said, 'There is no hope anywhere, and no sound and no promise. So now I know that there is nothing that can save me. I don't believe, and I don't know anything at all. But without faith or hope, in the utmost despair, I swear to You that I will never drink again. And I know that that can't be true unless You are.'

Then I got into bed and slept.

I had had no feeling of hope. I felt myself received by total silence: not even that, there was nothing to receive anything. I had no sense of anything 'there' at all.

And in the morning I awoke, feeling desperately ill, and all that day I felt ill and weak from the drunkenness of the day before. But towards evening I suddenly realized that I was walking in tranquillity and with perfect confidence; and that tranquillity and assurance has never left me. (Except in dreams; I still sometimes dream that I have put on chains again.)

There, then, is the 'crisis'. Now that it is written down I can see that there is nothing in it to prevent most readers from going to get the brown paper and string and hurrying to catch the second post, so that the library may send down something better worth the trouble of their attention.

I shall be sorry if all readers do this; but as no one can be sure what readers will do until, at least, the book is printed and in circulation, and as, to be printed, a book must first be written, I shall continue to write it, and now, at last, begin at the beginning.

I was born, then, in May 1906, in London. The house in which I was born is rather an ugly one, standing in a street of similar houses which runs somewhere between Bond Street and Hyde Park. My father was fairly rich, although I never realized it nor had occasion to; for most of our acquaintances were richer, and both my parents had – for different reasons – a superstitious fear of money which made them always afraid to believe in their fortune, and even while they were living luxuriously and spending considerable sums of money, they always worried about finances and complained of poverty. So that, while in fact I was being educated at a most expensive public school for young ladies and having such 'extras' as riding, violin lessons, swimming lessons as a Junior Member of the Bath Club, and was the sole charge of a highly-trained nurse who received a yearly allowance from which to feed and dress me; all this time I was hearing talk about things we could not afford, and things I must not hope for, and the great anxiety my parents felt about 'how we should manage' to meet this and that expense.

As a result of this, and of the incredible fact that I was given, from the age of about five to eight, *1*d. *a week* pocket-money (which of course had to be put in the church collection) and then, until I was ten or eleven, *3*d. *a week* (and I was at school during this time, of course), and after eleven, although I was raised to 6d. a week, I did not have any chance to learn about the management of money, I have been crippled so far as matters of finance are concerned, and the whole subject of money is one (to me) of the wildest fantasy and totally unreal. Nor have I ever managed to learn how to keep it, or how to possess it without fear, and it is only with the greatest difficulty that I avoid becoming extremely mean, so far as the giving away of actual *money* is concerned. I can spend money, turn it into objects, and give away the objects with complete ease – with too much ease. But giving away a coin or a note is a painful effort and I suppose always will be.

I was sickly as a child, I think. Unfortunately my mother had the reputation of being a 'malade imaginaire'. I was too young to know this for some time and during that time of course I believed in all her illnesses and she used to describe her sufferings to me very often – sufferings not only physical. She would tell me about all the things that troubled her in our domestic life: my father's saturnine moods; his lack of understanding; my sister's harsh tongue and difficult temperament; the servants' touchiness and the many miseries felt by a sensitive character such as, she told me, I had inherited from her.

Certainly I was often ill, although I did not have all the sicknesses than ran through the school. I had bronchitis badly; I had influenza when I was a small baby, and almost died of it; I had tonsils and adenoids out, in an operation done at home; and when I was nine I had an appendicitis, also dealt with at home. Between these operations I had influenza again several times, and chicken-pox. But I cannot remember that I had any other major sicknesses to account for the many times I was absent from school on the grounds of ill health: and when,

44

slightly later on, my sister (who was eight years older than I) told me that I was nothing but a hypocritical little 'malade imaginaire', *just like our mother*, it gave me, so to speak, a shock to realize that it did not shock me –

My mother was also very devout. She was a High Anglican and I was brought up in this faith. I had an innocent and truthful religion myself, for some years; I believe until I was about eleven, when I was confirmed. My sister, meanwhile (who was away at boarding-school) went through a period of extreme devotion, first to the same faith and then to that faith identified with one of the mistresses at her school. However, when she returned for the holidays, aged about seventeen–eighteen, she was beginning to be disillusioned and what was then called 'cynical and introspective'. This affected me considerably, because she 'persecuted' me. At first I embraced martyrdom and even when she belaboured me with arguments and blasphemies (which genuinely shocked and frightened me) I put up quite a fierce fight and time and again stood up to considerable violence – not always only in words. But her grown-up and 'modern' shrewdness, together with my mother's dreadfully sentimental 'pi-talk' (which caused me increasing agonies of embarrassment) undermined my own security and in a short time I could not find anything to believe in.

I must have been an attractive small child, to some people, and remarkably repulsive to others. I was naturally docile and gentle, and I think perhaps I was brave when I began. But my nurse (who had sole charge of me every day and every night, except for some Sundays when my mother would take me out) was extremely sharp and bullying. She was like those small terrier dogs which rear up into a fight with every beast that passes, and snap at every leg within reach. Her voice was sharp and high and she scolded incessantly; her hands were small and very hard and she used them freely. To see her brushing out her long, red-golden hair in the morning light was to know what savage, rancorous temper was contained – or not contained – in her small tight body. She slashed and struck at her own head, while her little bright pale blue eyes ranged about the room, seeing everything at once but eternally suspicious of the some thing, the one thing, they might have missed –

But I can remember being attractive to people; I can remember the warm feeling of reciprocation – how love flooded into me from them and flowed out again to them. Not only as a very young child (for I expect all very young children have this sensation) but right on into double figures I remember it. And 'double-figures' reminds me of the strange bitter feeling I had when, on a Sunday morning in May, when my nurse and I were solemnly walking in what was then called 'Church Parade', a lady who knew my mother and who stopped to speak to me asked how old I was, and when I said 'Ten in two days' time,' she shook her head and said 'Oh dear, you go into double figures then, and you'll never get back again!' I remember, too, that although this observation filled me with awe and made me pensive for a time, I took to boasting, repeatedly and whenever I had the least opportunity, of 'Now I am in double-figures,' as if it were a personal accomplishment.

The pleasure I got from loving people was genuine and not adulterated with vanity or greed, at any rate for some time. I have always felt this pleasure very keenly (and really I do not think that it has become bad; I need not have talked about adulteration in this connection). The pleasure of being loved very soon became mingled with vanity and greed, but soonest with a passionate desire for security. I felt – I expressed it in so many words to myself very early in my life – that if only *one person* would love me, me particularly, peculiarly, me above all, then I would never be beaten by anything nor even fear anything in my life again. I quite believed this, and when I was very young I tried to bring back – if not to life, yet to a visible presence – my mother's brother who had died when he was seven.

Robin's portrait hung in my mother's room, I think. I used to visit it and stare and stare at the little solemn-faced boy (very much like me) wearing a black velvet coat and holding a sporting gun. There was no trace of a smile on his lips or in his eyes. He looked gravely always, and I looked sorrowfully back at him and thought that if only I could conjure his ghost back to be with me (I did not think 'to play with me') I would love him best of all, and he would love me best of all, and we would be safe so. I deliberately tried to force his presence into visibility; just as, a few years later, I spent almost the whole Easter holidays in trying to persuade myself that I believed in my Guardian Angel. If I could have believed, I knew, then my longing to have one person to love absolutely, who would love me absolutely, would be forever satisfied; safely satisfied, too, because that particular relationship, obviously, could not be 'cut in on' and would not be destroyed by death. But I could not make it real. I only had it at all when I was exerting all my inward powers (whatever they were: mysterious, undefined, hard to remember from one time to the next how to get at them, how to use them, but undeniably real and effective; not only in childhood, but up to this present time).

At school I was shy and nothing ever became real to me. School was never real-life. The other children were both frightening and to be scorned. I never believed that I could do anything as well as they did it and yet I am sure that I always felt superior to them. In fact, I could do most things that they did; I was fairly equal with the rest of my class in most subjects and much better than the rest in one or two; at games I was good; at music I was good when I was alone with the teacher and hopeless (as I was in everything) if it was a question of public performance. I could not even stand up and answer in my turn in class without suffering something very much like anguish. But I could do mental arithmetic, write papers at great speed, answer written questions and so on with ease and often much more successfully than most of the others. But if a question required me to stand up and give a verbal answer I was usually so dazzled, as it were, by the fact that I would have to become conspicuous and speak aloud that I did not begin even to understand the question. And that is how I am today.

I brought back one or two friends from school; they had tea with me or we met at picnics in the Park in the summer. Occasionally I was positively forced by my parents or my nurse to go out to tea at their houses. I was shy, silent and uncooperative, and always left these occasions with a sense of complete failure. But I did not quarrel, unless it was absolutely forced on me; and I did not put up any creditable fight against oppression after I was about ten years old; but I used to lose all my fear (which was not, I think, physical fear but self-consciousness and a pathological degree of shyness) if it was a question of standing up for someone else who was being oppressed. This I could do, and it gave me a

48

wonderful sense of liberation and gaiety, too, on the rare occasions that came my way.

The 1914–18 War spread over my childhood. It began when I was eight, the first year I went to school, and ended when I was twelve. We stayed in London all the time, and went as usual to our country house on the East Coast for the holidays. It was thought brave, if not foolhardy, in the sort of society we met, to persist in going to the East Coast; and so I got a kind of superficial boastfulness about Zeppelins and German warships, especially after the sea-bombardment of one of the Norfolk coast towns which, nine miles from our own house on the coast, was near enough to be exciting and to make a good story.

The boastfulness *was* superficial, and I knew it. I knew that I was a coward and I tried very hard not to be. During the week of air-raids on London, my nursery being almost at the top of our tall house, I was wakened every night and brought downstairs to the supposedly safe room, which in daytime was the patients' waiting-room. Most of the people from neighbouring 'poor' houses used to shelter in the cellars of an hotel nearby, and our servants went over there too. We scorned them for that, supposing they did it out of pure cowardice, but in fact they went because there was good company and the hotel gave them hot drinks and delicious food. One night, however, one of the young women from a nearby slum-street, with her two-year-old little boy in her arms, battered on our front-door because, on her way to the hotel, she had been frightened by a bomb falling nearby and ours was the first door she found.

My father brought her in to the waiting-room with the rest of us, and the noise of the anti-aircraft guns was very loud just then (a small gun on a trolley ran up and down our street during every raid, firing all the time). I felt my knees shaking, a sign I knew well and was ashamed of. I decided to be very brave. And so I went out and went upstairs in the dark, up past the drawing-room floor, the parents' floor, and on up the twisting dark stairs to my own nursery where I snatched up a toy and ran desperately downstairs again, and as I went past the window on the stairs I saw the great flash and sweep of searchlights and felt terrified. And so reached the waiting-room (of course no one had missed me) and gave the child the toy.

I hoped, I suppose, that this was brave and would be commended. No one had noticed, so I had to tell them. No one was impressed. And it had not cured me of cowardice, as I had really thought it would. My knees trembled in all the other air-raids, and indeed, they trembled when guns fired in Madrid, when bombs fell in Valencia, whenever I found myself in a war again. I know now that I am a coward, quite grotesquely a coward. There is more to tell about this, but nothing to say in my own defence, for my life has been neither more nor less hazardous than anyone else's, and I do not expect I have been more afraid than most people are. I am simply totally unable to master my fear. There cannot be any acceptable excuse for this, and I am bitterly ashamed of it.

Out of my window at this moment I can see two young rabbits who have come out to feed on the meadow across the river. They start, they sit upright, with ears erect, at every noise or stirring of the hedge behind them. But their fears quieten and after a second or two they are down again and feeding placidly enough. I watch them humbly, but I am never able to learn the way of it.

When I lived (it is a much later, a much happier, part of my story) in a manor house in Norfolk, I remember making a determined effort to overcome cowardice by reason, by knowledge, by attentive learning. I read Marcus Aurelius; I read stories of the 'last' war (this was in 1933), and that war had already its quality of profound tragedy and beauty which I think it will never lose; all accounts of it, in poetry and prose, brought crowding back the million ghosts, all young as it seemed, all brave and all dead. It was the right place to go for lessons in courage; and one evening I spent perhaps an hour of long summer twilight, watching the behaviour of a marauding tom-cat who was raiding our house for food. He was ragged and lean but he was matchlessly brave. It was an exhibition of infinite cunning and tenacity as he worked his way through the shrubbery, along the stable wall, and at last ventured himself across the open space to the kitchen door. He was not very large, he was shabby and he had a crippled foreleg, but he braved all the hostility of a strange house, dogs and tame cats, servants, people with guns, and the noises of dinner preparing. I could see his bright, watchful eyes as he turned his head this way and that and pricked his ragged ears to listen. And then with his swiftly-limping, sliding run he was into the house and out again with a large piece of fish from the house-cats' bowl.

After he had vanished again in the shrubbery I sat back on my heels and tried to impress that image on my mind. And succeeded, for I can see it plainly still, and understand it; but I cannot copy it.

To return, briefly, to childhood: Kierkegaard describes what, perhaps, made me also lonely and estranged. He says: 'But when one is a child ... and then, in spite of the fact that one is a child ... then to be a spirit! Frightful torture!' And goes on, further down the same paragraph, 'In the two ages of immediacy, childhood and youth,

51

I ... helped myself out ... by some sort of counterfeit, and not being quite clear myself about the talents bestowed upon me, I suffered the pains of not being like others – which naturally at that period I would have given everything to be able to be, if only for a short time ... '

That is one aspect, and it is perfectly true that I too felt just so. But although I was sometimes quite genuinely aware of 'being a spirit', many uglier things came to overwhelm my consciousness, and a crude boastfulness, a more subtle self-aggrandizement by way of humility, an unpleasant, pretentious air of mystery and trouble: these I wore more and more often, and used them as it were to excuse my isolation. I used them to ensure it, that is true, but also to justify it to myself. Airs of superior wisdom, even of esoteric knowledge, I wore before the children I could not avoid asking home to tea. And this was successful; it saved me from intimacy with them which, I thought, was what I wanted.

I was happy, during holidays in our Norfolk house, when the boy stayed with me. He was a year younger than I, a kind, witty, inventive boy, who felt some friendship for me and infinite friendship for the place I lived in and the pleasures I could command. We went out for whole days alone together, building elaborate sand fortresses or bracken cabins on the dunes; we played tennis and bicycle polo; we ate fruit of all kinds in the garden and hot-houses; we sailed boats on the Broads; we went out for excursions in the family car. Undoubtedly he loved these holidays and I did too; but I was never completely at ease unless I was alone – and even alone I was not often *at ease*: I was often in ecstasy.

By myself I climbed trees. I 'owned' three tall trees in our grounds, and very high in each of these I had nailed boards to act as tables, and on one of them a large crucifix. I would pray and meditate for hours together, while I was still in that state of mind; and later I would take my small chess-set up one or other tree, and work busily away at problems from a book. And later still I took my flute up the tree with me and practised (very unsuccessfully). Or with a pair of field-glasses I watched birds and wrote long pages of 'observations' on their habits. And all the time, for as long as I can remember, I wrote verses, rhymed and unrhymed, and composed the words and tunes of songs which I sang to myself and, I would think, 'To God – '

I remember that during one summer when I was ten or eleven, I used to conceal paper and pencil in the hollow handlebars of my bicycle, and go off across the flat country towards the Broads, and sit in a field and write poetry, or eloquent letters to imaginary people. My sister somehow discovered these and taunted me, assuring me that she would always know where I hid my 'works', hide I never so cleverly.

This filled me with terror. And then I had the idea of sawing off the tip of a small celluloid crucifix and putting a roll of poems in the hollow shaft of the cross. I thought that even if she did suspect this, she might feel it better not to pry into the shaft of the cross. I do not know why I thought this, and of course I was wrong, for she did pry and she did find, and she made a great speech to me about the 'sacrilege' of defacing such a holy object, and the crass blasphemy of using it to hide my really dreadful poems in.

My sister must have been about nineteen then. From that time until she was twenty-four or twenty-five she showed the utmost diligence and resourcefulness in tracking me down. It was impossible to keep any secret from her or to have anything that she did not read. And I was already a coward. There was little difference between me and an idiot all that time, so far as I can judge from the extraordinarily stupid things I did in my efforts to escape her. All the time, too, I was verging on loving her; I would have sudden collapses into confidence and an unpleasant kind of clinging, miserable dependence on her. All through my early adolescence (which started, so far as physical symptoms are concerned, when I was thirteen) my sister dominated my life, and always as a threat, a dread, even though occasionally she would suddenly become kind – or apparently kind – and 'draw me out' to tell her my strange fancies, my longings, my ambitions. But I never told her any fear, because she was the centre of every fear I had – and God knows I had many.

When I remember myself at this age, it seems to me that I had lost almost all independence of character; I had collapsed, as it were, and would not (perhaps could not?) exert myself to put out any shoots or tendrils; but just lay along the ground, scarcely feeling any movement towards getting on with being alive.

A little earlier it had not been so bad; if, indeed, I had shown any signs of this weakness at all. I remember something that happened while I was still a fervent Anglo-Catholic child. A schoolfriend was staying with me, elder sister to the little boy who came each year. She was a child of positive, domineering character, ill-tempered, attractive and spoilt. She had a lame leg and one afternoon I had managed to haul her up onto the flat roof of the house – a dangerous proceeding, even by oneself, and strictly forbidden by my father. But he was not there then; I must have wheedled permission from my in-attentive mother, I suppose, for I rarely flatly disobeyed. However that may be, we had climbed there and sat on the

54

leads, conversing. And the child, who was a Scot and who had an extremely good, serious, Presbyterian nurse, was crossly arguing with me about the Saints. She hated them, she said; and didn't I carry the image of one in my pocket? What was that but an idol?

Now, it was true; I did carry a small flat wooden image of St Bernardino, my birthday saint, always in my pocket. And slept with it at night, too. For some reason I became combative and argued back, and when the child said angrily that she supposed I liked that nasty graven image better than I liked her, I produced it and gazed at it with irritating devotion and replied that indeed, I did love it much better than her.

She snatched the image from me and flung it as far as she could. It went right over the gutter and dropped on to the gravel below.

I got up slowly and stood over her, and I can remember feeling astonished at the thing I said, and the solemnity with which I said it. I told her that if the image were broken she would live to be very sorry for it; a very dreadful thing would happen to her, I said; she had better prepare herself – and then I clambered down to the ground and picked up my saint, perfectly intact.

Now, I had had no idea of uttering such mysterious and dreadful threats; nor had I any idea of what I would do when I got back to the roof-top. But when I saw her sitting there, her eyes dark with superstitious fear, I did the most curious thing. The image was back in my pocket. She asked if it was all right, and I replied slowly and impressively, 'I shan't tell you. You can wait and see – '

She was extremely frightened. I knew that and I rejoiced. It is a curious thing; I cannot understand it and I find it hard to believe that I did behave like that, because I was extremely susceptible to other people's feelings and caught their sensations vividly and immediately. I loathed frightening people and I was embarrassed by feeling a sense of power. It would, for instance, have been perfectly simple for me to have stayed on the ground and refused to help her get down from the roof. It is the kind of thing a teasing or angry child does do. But I could never have done that; it would have seemed unfair, I think, and certainly would have embarrassed me. But so far as I remember I did not feel any scruples at all about this bullying. And I let her go to bed without removing the curse. I went to bed myself, quite serenely, but soon after that her nurse fetched my nurse, who fetched me, and I was taken into her bedroom to undo the curse, because she had worked herself into a frenzy of fear and would not lie down to sleep. So, reluctantly I think, I showed her the idol, intact, and presumably she went peacefully to sleep; and so did I. And I do not think there were any repercussions next day.

That was independent action, with a vengeance; but a year or so later I had become practically incapable of it, unless carried out by stealth, deceitfully and slyly, with a sense of sickening distaste for myself, and with absolutely no self-confidence at all. I always knew I should be caught, and I knew I should collapse under questioning, and I always was and I always did. Besides which, my 'independent actions' were always pointless – or came to seem so directly I had undertaken them. They were usually connected with puerile games of imagination, games too young for my age, games in which I pretended to be something very silly and unbelieved-in; a red Indian, or a general. At eleven or so a girl-child has outgrown these games, and I had; but I tried to take refuge in them, and I gave myself away every time by such stupidities as

cutting signs on trees which my sister would invariably
see; or writing ridiculous 'Orders of the Day' or
'Despatches' which she would at once find and thrust in
front of me – often at tea or in front of her grown-up
friends, with gibes at my childish handwriting and
grandiose language. I suffered extremities of pain and
shame at these exposures, only to be caught out again.
And at this period I began to have dreadul nightmares and
to walk in my sleep.

Towards the end of these holidays, my mother was
going away and I was to be left in charge of my sister and a
Belgian refugee girl who had been at school with her and
who was now acting as my 'governess'. This girl was
painfully ugly, with a long hatchet-chin and thick
unpleasant black hair and a dirty brown skin which shone
with grease. I feared and loathed her, but it was entirely
my fault that she had come to us. My sister had told me
stories of her tragic life and when my nurse had been
dismissed at last (that is a story in itself) the idea had
unfortunately come to me that Mariette might like to have
the job and I had suggested it. At the time everyone had
thought it such a good idea that I had felt very happy,
because they applauded it and it seemed to me I had been
very kind and very contriving.

But Mariette had a passionate, a desperate devotion to
my sister. I knew nothing of this until after she had
arrived. My sister, I think, had encouraged it at first but by
now she was sick of it and was treating Mariette austerely.
As a result my life was made extremely miserable and I was
in a state of bewilderment. Nothing I could do was right.
Mariette had, of course, adopted my sister's theory that she
was less favoured than I, and as a consequence Mariette
hated me and 'took me down' whenever she could. I

became afraid of her. She was a malevolent poor creature, anyway, and her black uncomely visage horrified me, and I hated her smell, and her thick accent, and the vague pornography of her jokes and allusions. She spent most days writing notes or letters to my sister, or waiting for the post, or haunting the room my sister used as a studio, and whenever they had a scene Mariette would return to me, in black rage, black melancholy, floods of tears, and nothing I could say or do would ease her, nor could I feel any depth of pity for her, and that troubled my conscience deeply.

One night, I do not know why, just after my mother had gone away, my sister and I were sleeping together in my mother's big bed. I have no idea why this was; it was extremely unusual. I had been put to bed early, with a nightlight burning, and I awoke to hear screams and find my sister fallen across me as I lay in bed; and the room flickering and shining from a flame that burned, apparently, all along one side of it.

In fact, the nightlight had caught its paper wrapper, and my sister had wakened and thought the room on fire, and had put her hand, palm downwards, on the flame. The pain of the hot wax burning her had made her half-faint.

She stammered out that she had been saving my life and I climbed out of bed and ran to fetch Mariette, who came into the room in her long nightdress, moaning and exclaiming while my sister cried in anguish and begged us to do something quickly. I remember that I ran into the dining-room and got the bottle of olive oil and poured that on her hand. And Mariette hastened downstairs and woke the old cook, who loathed her and refused to do anything to help, but said we were all making a great deal too much noise. Mariette then fetched some cold boiled potatoes from the larder and applied them as a cover, and they eased the pain considerably, and all the rest of the night she and I applied them as fresh dressings, and in the early morning sent the chauffeur to the village doctor some miles away. A telegram was sent to my mother, who returned that night. Meanwhile, Mariette spent all her spare time in reproaching and reviling me because my sister had got burned in trying to save me – and when my mother returned she too, I thought, seemed to blame me because my sister had sacrificed herself for me.

I hung about very miserably, trying to help and hoping for praise because I had thought of the salad oil ... My father praised me, when he came; but Mariette's angry reproaches went on and never slackened all through that horrible summer until, at the end of it, she was politely dismissed. Not because she was unsuitable to have charge of me but because her devotion to my sister made her unbearable to the whole household.

This incident weighed me down very much. I suffered a great deal of remorseful love for my sister, who had herself suffered so much pain for me. She must love me very much, I thought, and I had come so near to hating her. I knew that she had cause for jealousy of me; I knew that she tormented herself because of me. I felt it was my fault and I did not know how to remedy it. And she had made me despise and loathe myself, and most times feel myself to be beneath contempt. Occasionally, it is true, I swung to the other extreme and felt violently sanctimonious and self-righteous. But that was uncomfortable too, for inwardly I knew quite well that it had no justification in fact.

The next year I had someone else in charge of me; this time too she was my choice and my fault and she was horrible. A small, very pale creature with a face like an

59

earwig. Her name was 'Blossom' and there could not have been a more unsuitable name. She was the first servant to adore my sister and she 'took her side' so sharply that, for the first time, it became, as it were, official that there were two camps in the house and that my sister was the oppressed and neglected child, while I was spoilt, smug and intolerable. I feared and hated Blossom, who had singular gifts of bullying and sneaking. If I could have had a clear run of hating her it might have been all right, but here again compassion hamstrung me. Blossom was engaged to a local man who jilted her. I was going upstairs, in the town house, when the telegram in which he announced his intention of breaking their engagement was given to Blossom. She fell flat down on the polished floor in a dead faint. And I nearly collapsed from shock myself. I remember my father, angry and impatient at being fetched from a patient, saying that it was only a faint and she must pull herself together. I loathed him for such dreadful inhumanity. But he had loathed Blossom for her miss-ish ways and pale, earwig face; and perhaps he knew instinctively that she was full of dirty pruderies and a particularly unpleasant brand of indecent conversation.

That summer, while Blossom was with us, I remember that my mother was to go away from the Norfolk house, leaving me with my sister and the maid. I dreaded her going so much that I fretted myself into a vague illness. As the car was at the door to take her to the station, I heard my mother say that she must take my temperature and if it was up she would not go. Left with the thermometer in my mouth, in panic in case I had no fever, I suddenly thought of a plan, and pressed the thermometer against the hot-water bottle for a second or two, and then replaced it. Of course, when they looked at it, it registered 110 degrees ...

It was obvious that I had somehow caused it to go up, but I denied that stoutly. My sister then demanded that I should swear on the Bible that I hadn't made it go up. I quailed, but swore. However, my mother simply looked uncomfortable, and said she expected I would be all right. And went away. Soon after she had gone I was told to get up and, in disgrace with fortune and men's eyes, I did so.

Two or three days later, I still felt unwell. Blossom had decided to wash my hair (which was then long) and I, with a headache, begged to be let off. But she invoked my sister who said that I was a dirty little brute (at that time I neglected my hands and nails and was inclined to be dirty, it is true) and although I begged her to let me off, she insisted that it should be washed, and it duly was.

That evening I developed an extraordinarily sharp pain in my back and could scarcely breathe. The doctor, called in a hurry, said I had a severe attack of pleurisy and my parents must be sent for. They were at a theatre in London and were summoned from there, and caught the night train down. I was very ill for some time, and it hurt considerably.

My sister suffered agonies of remorse. She accused herself of having caused my illness; she haunted my room and gave up most of her time to drawing me pictures, reading to me, bringing me presents. I, in my turn, suffered agonies of remorse as well! I had again come near hating her; I had misjudged her; she really loved me deeply and I had thought her a brute and a bully. Each separately, we suffered this and that but never came into anything like intimacy or friendship. It was an over-strained, tormented household, the two or us going through pangs of remorse, my mother suffering (and freely communicating) her own peculiar sensitivity and religious fervour, my father having bouts of rebellion against this unpleasant family he had cumbered himself with, and disliking my sister because he thought her graceless and ill-mannered, and telling her so sometimes, which did not make matters any easier.

By now, the War had ended. My sister went to Belgium to stay with Mariette's family. I returned to school in London. I worked hard and harder; all my days were spent in work. Competition was fierce and I scarcely understood a thing I was doing, but I passed all exams very well and got excellent, even outstanding reports. All this time, at every moment I could, I read and wrote poetry, read and wrote essays – never stories – and held theological discussions with myself, which at last swung me from faith to unfaith.

I had been confirmed when I was eleven. I spent most of the night before my confirmation in prayer, and most of the night before my first communion in prayer too. I had a vision of St Hugh of Lincoln, or a dream perhaps, just before I was confirmed. And the bishop who confirmed me (whom I had not seen before) had the face of the saint in my dream. I never quite remembered what St Hugh said to me, except that it had seemed to me that he greeted me, recognized me, received me as if I were someone he loved and had expected; and I had it in my mind for a long time, as a kind of misty certainty, that *something* he had said was a promise that I should be very good.

And I did want to be. I wanted that more than anything else but very very close to it came the desire to be *known to be good*. Not specifically to be praised for it, but that it should be positively known by everyone, so that I myself should not be able to doubt it. It is hard to explain more clearly than that, but it is an intrinsic part of my life, this desire for confirmation and supporting evidence; it is everything I feel and do, although latterly it seems to have settled into something like serenity. Not into resignation, nothing at all like that; but into the serenity one might perhaps achieve when at long last one had got used to having a maimed limb or one blind eye.

[II]

I remember too many details if I try to tell this story chronologically. Perhaps it will be better to ignore time and use space as if it were all mine; as indeed it is, at any rate in retrospect.

Time has always been pliable, so far as I am concerned. Throughout my life there have been curious 'side-slips', inexplicable but perfectly authentic. One happened yesterday. I was packing up a parcel of books to go back to the London Library, and I wrote my name on the space provided on the label. As I did so I thought – for no reason at all – 'Supposing this label goes to Edith Sitwell, and she reads my name ... ' and then I thought 'But that couldn't happen; she goes to the Library for her books, I expect, and doesn't have them posted.' Finishing the parcel I started to tidy remnants of paper and on one of them, which I certainly had not looked at before, was an old London Library label, and in the space provided for the Sender's Name was written 'Miss Edith Sitwell, D.Litt: Litt:D.'

That is a digression. So is this: sometime in 1930, I believe, I went in the morning to visit someone who, only a little later on, I began to love deeply and who has been my dearest love ever since. It was one of those brief periods in which I seemed to have succeeded, and I had not drunk any alcohol for many days. In her house as we talked, she offered me a tiny glass of Cassis liqueur, and I refused it; but she had poured it out and she persuaded me. I drank it and thanked her and, the conversation ended, I went back to my mother's flat where I was to have lunch.

The spell was broken, for it took only that slight pressure to snap my self-control; I ordered some wine for lunch, and while I was drinking it I was called to the telephone. She spoke to me urgently: 'I am glad you are all right. I was afraid something might have happened to you on the way home. After you had gone I was washing up the glasses and as I took hold of the one you had used, *I felt your hand* on it – it was as if I were clasping your hand and not the glass at all. I was afraid it portended some catastrophe.'

As I put down the receiver I was very much afraid. It *did* portend a catastrophe, I thought; and so indeed it did, although a slow one and so long drawn-out that we did not recognize it as such. For many many things have been spoilt, many things wasted, many extravagancies committed and disgraces brought about because of that deadly weakness; and she has been affected by them all, since that day; and nothing that I say of this is exaggerated.

Since I have decided to ignore time continuity, I can revert here to my early childhood, to tell of an incident that I remembered when I saw a weasel in the road, as I went to work yesterday. It was when I was about eight years old, and dressed in fancy-dress to go to a birthday party. My nurse had designed the costume and I was to be a weasel. I had some kind of furry brown back and hood, with a long tail of beaver fur, I remember, and my white chest was made of cotton-wool. As we went along the passage, led by the butler who had a cab waiting outside, my father opened the door of his consulting room and looked out. I stopped to be admired, and was horrified to see his face change and become very angry. He turned to my nurse and ordered her to take off that cotton-wool; something else must be substituted, he said; that stuff was too inflammable: there might easily be a disaster. My nurse was furious, naturally, and I was dragged upstairs and subjected to a great deal of pulling and pushing and at last some sort of white material was sewn on instead of the wool. We arrived at the party late, and I was aware that I did not look nearly as nice as I had been at first, and I felt shy and unhappy. But towards the end of the party, sure enough, someone set fire to me ... a lighted match or something was tossed against my white chest, and the stuff was scorched and marked, but it did not flare up as the cotton-wool would have done.

I do not remember being very much impressed by this occurrence. I believe I was not really surprised. All my life through I have not so much 'believed in' second sight, premonitions and so forth as found them quite unsurprising, although I have never found any way of inducing them; I wish I had.

There is that 'second sight' and there is also another experience which I think one can call 'intimation'. It is a curious sensation, a feeling of recognition, perhaps; not recognition of something known before but recognition of the importance (usually the symbolical importance) of something apparently trivial which has just happened. Here is an instance; it occurred at about the same time as the affair of the glass, told above.

I was waiting in the car outside that same house; while I sat there, in the London street, a violent rain storm broke and the rain drops dashed themselves against the bonnet and windscreen of the car. As I was watching them I saw a crane fly had been blown against the glass of the windscreen and was being battered by the large rain drops.

He slipped down on to the bonnet of the car and there was beaten and battered and half-drowned by the rain. Ordinarily compassion would have made me get out and try to rescue him; but this time I watched because I had to: I was under a kind of cold compulsion – for a moment or two I did not understand it, but as the house door opened and the person I was waiting for came out, in the bustle of getting him into the car and loading in luggage and waving good-bye, I realized sharply and beyond any doubt that the storm and the crane fly were in some inescapable sense symbolical; that the crane fly, fragile and helpless and savagely struggling, was my spirit, and the storm that overwhelmed it was a type of the horror that, I knew with despair, was overwhelming me.

These are sick fancies, perhaps not worth retelling. But a life is made up of these minute incidents, fancies, intuitions and intimations; so small and so numerous that they are almost impossible to distinguish apart, once they have been built in to the pattern, once they have been cemented one to another by having been experienced. And to extract one here and there, to point out this fragment and that and remember how it looked before it became integrated to the whole, that is one way of setting down an account of a life.

At the time of this incident I was twenty-four. In the twelve years or so between then and the reigns of Mariette and Blossom I had done a great many things; and I had done them – they had not just happened to me. When I remember back I am struck by the curious strenuousness of the way I lived my life in those years; and yet all the time I was in a daze; wholly conscious of certain things (vividly aware of sensations, of intimations, moods, the feelings set in motion by poetry and music) but walking in a dream in all my exterior life. I was desperately and intensely happy to myself, by myself, but I was lost and very frightened as well, all the time.

Desire for someone who would love me protectingly had led me into a strange, stiff courtship with a schoolboy who came to our East Anglian village for his holidays. I do not remember how we came to the arrangement, but it was settled that we should be married as soon as possible, and that we should write love letters to each other, and think of each other at six o'clock every evening. This went on for about two years and then, in 1918 I think, he fell into disgrace at his public school and was expelled. I did not know until later that this was for homosexuality. I would not have understood it. He stayed a night with us in London on his way to the docks, where he was to take ship for Java, where his parents lived. My father expressed a violent distaste for the boy (whom he had liked before) and this surprised me. He gave orders that I was not to see him alone, my mother told me, but nevertheless she allowed him to come into my room and say good-bye in the early morning of his departure. I was tormented by shyness, which absorbed me completely. The evening before I had been alone with him for half-an-hour or so, in the billiard room of our house, a room I loved, to which no one ever came. The boy (he was about seventeen then) asked me to sit on his lap and I perched myself there, stiffly and uncomfortably, and sat erect, and after a little while got down again. But when he came to say good-bye he bent over my bed and kissed me on the lips, and I kissed him.

This engagement (for so we called it) lasted on, so far as letter writing went. Meanwhile, at my father's golf club, I made friends with a shy, very ugly, young man of thirty-two. The War had just ended and he had been demobilized from the Naval Air Service. He was more valuable and dear to me than anyone had ever been. He gave me books – Boswell's *Life of Johnson*, Lamb's *Essays, Omar Khayyam* – he talked to me about music; he taught me to play chess; he taught me to see that trains running across the dark country at night, with flames coming from the funnel and the lighted windows making a long bright dragon over the fenland, were beautiful and not – as I had been brought up to think – ugly and unromantic machines spoiling the face of Nature. He loved me, I think, and perhaps thought ahead to the time when I should grow up. His parents asked my parents whether they might take me abroad for a time, but I was so shy that when I heard of this I implored them not to allow it. If it had happened, everything else in my life would have been different, but I do not in the least regret it, except that I wish I might have experienced that life too.

In 1919, at Christmas time, we went to Italy. My father was beginning to be ill, and I had been very ill with colitis and was on a strict diet. We had just moved from the house in Mayfair to a service flat in Westminster. It was a very different life, much freer, and I enjoyed it.

We travelled over in bad weather, and in Italy it was fine and warm. My father bathed on Christmas Day, I remember, but I was not allowed to.

We stayed in Italy until May. My parents went back to London in March or April and left me in the charge of my sister (than twenty-one). At the hotel I had fallen in love for the first time in my life, for although I loved the schoolboy, and deeply loved the young man, I never felt overwhelmed and swept away and intoxicated until this year in Italy. I fell in love with a tall, beautiful young woman who had large grey eyes and cloudy dark hair and

69

a low-pitched voice; her large white hands were rather clumsy but very caressing and she was perfectly used to being loved. She was rather silly and very emotional, and in her turn loved my sister with a perfectly normal, very devoted and sentimental passion. But she encouraged me. She wrote me notes and gave me flowers and keepsakes; I confided in her that I wrote poetry and she assured me that I was remarkable. I was exceedingly childish just then, I think, because I distinctly remember deciding that I must 'have' her, and although I did not know what this meant, I arranged with myself that I would return to England and grow older and then run away, dress as a man, emerge as one and meet her again, and marry her. That done, I would explain the circumstances to her and she would not mind at all, nor would we ever tell anyone else. We would live together in perfect happiness until we died – together.

Meanwhile, my sister (in her usual fashion) knew more or less what was going on in my head (although I do not think she ever knew this particular plan) and lost no opportunity of tormenting me about it. When my parents had left she exercised her authority and sent me to bed early every evening. While they had been there I sat up late and on most evenings I had danced with this girl, and then she had visited me in my bedroom and sat on my bed and read poetry to me, and told me mysterious anecdotes of her life. Now I was sent off to bed while the hotel people danced in the salon below, and later I would hear my sister come to bed, in the room opposite mine, and the girl come to *her* room, and I would lie in my bed and grieve bitterly and fruitlessly, and only very rarely she would come in to see me, and then she stayed only for a short time, and obviously fretted to be away.

It was a sharp initiation into love, and it bit quite deeply

70

into my heart; I strove very hard against my eating jealousy, and I was ashamed of it, too. But I did not defeat it.

The next year was spent in reading, and trying to write love poems.

The next year, 1922, I was sent to Paris with the girl I threatened with the curse of my wooden saint. She was now either sixteen or seventeen, and in some ways much more sophisticated than I. At fifteen I knew very little of the world I was sent out to see. I went with my head packed with little patchwork pieces of knowledge; I took with me, so far as I remember, Plato's *Republic*, the *Oxford Book of English Verse*, J. C. Squire's *Anthology of Modern Verse* (the first, green volume, containing Flecker, Edward Thomas, de la Mare, Robert Frost ... I *think* Robert Frost ...) Mandeville's *Travels, Towards Democracy* by Edward Carpenter, and almost as soon as I was there I got the *Oxford Book of French Verse* and set to work to write poems after the manner of Verlaine. The girl I was with took no books but a Bible and a little paper book of daily reading from the Bible.

We clung together at first; we were homesick and frightened of the three middle-aged sisters, the Mademoiselles de Rigny, with whom we lived. They kept a small house, at 9 rue Ybry, Neuilly-sur-Seine. There was Mlle de Rigny herself, with a scanty fringe curled into brittle thin rolls every morning (and the smell of her scorched hair made us feel sick); Mlle Yvonne, who had a flat, pale, wicked face and understood, but would not speak, English; who listened at doors and read private letters and loathed us bitterly; and Mlle Germaine, who was shy, gauche, rather appealing in an ugly, affectionate way, and who suffered with her digestion and scattered

71

strange terracotta dust over all her food, from a packet which made us giggle because it had a large inscription announcing that it banished constipation. She died of cancer soon after, but while we were there she did not seem to be ill. She flushed very red after meals, we noticed, and yet ate very little and drank no wine. She went out early in the morning and it was whispered that she went to work in a shop somewhere. One of the English girls who was there with us (we knew her in London; she was very pretty and very rich) said that she would have to send a report of this rumour home to her father; he would not like her to stay on there, she said, if one of the women worked in a shop – or anywhere else, for that matter. They were supposed to be ladies, and if they were not, then they were taking her father's money on false pretences.

I was very much struck with this argument. I had never met outspoken snobbery before. She did, in fact, leave very shortly, but I do not remember whether it was for fear of contamination.

We were completely ignorant of the state of France, at that date just after the end of the War. Of course we knew that the Mlles de Rigny were poor, and we knew that they were very proud and that they kept a strict social code; but we did not think at all about how difficult it was for them to maintain their position and yet house us.

A young French woman came as Chaperon sometimes; she was called Mlle de Bergevain and she was handsome, tall, distinguished and modest. I came near to loving her and I felt an affection and a respect for her that I still feel whenever I remember her now. She liked me, I think, and took pains to show me pictures, and when she took us to galleries and museums, or to the Opéra, she kept me beside her and talked to me. I did not learn much, however; I was hampered by the accursed shyness and self-consciousness which I have always suffered; it distracted my attention and made me idiotic. But from her I did learn to read Anatole France, to buy cheap books about modern French painters and to read French literary reviews, which she lent me.

The curse of poverty still blighted me. I was allowed 10s. a week which was supposed to keep me in handkerchiefs, gloves, powder, hairdressing, stockings and stamps. I think – at the then rate of exchange – I had about 50–60 francs a week, therefore. It was an absurd sum. We were rather badly fed; the household was penurious and we were often hungry. That meant we bought biscuits and little cakes and chocolate, as well as miniature bottles of liqueurs which we drank at night in our bedrooms, having parties which we thought were desperate dissipations. I did not, in fact, attend many of these parties, because I thought them beneath me. I was being an Intellectual then. I spent ten francs or so on a plaster-of-Paris skull, laid on a plaster-of-Paris book; and with this in the centre of the table, and a candle on either side of it, using a purple quill pen and purple ink, I sat up until two or three in the morning, in the early spring of that year, writing poems in shaky French and eloquent English, and writing instalments of a grand serial story called (I did not know why) 'The Ravens', which I read aloud to my English friend, who complained because all the love passages petered out in a line of dots. They could not do otherwise. I did not know anything that could substitute for the dots.

In May 1922 I fell in love again.

[III]

Lana was three years older than me – even a little more. She was in her twentieth year. We considered this to be extraordinarily old. We felt chivalrously sorry for her. To have reached that great age and not to be engaged. My school friend knew that Lana was 'common' but I did not. I had scarcely any 'class-consciousness' then. I thought Lana frightening at first, because she was so old, because she could speak French accurately and fluently, with a charming accent, and because she curled her short-cut hair. This hair was beguiling; nut-brown, with golden hairs growing in a fine peak from her high forehead. She was very small and delicately made, and she dressed superbly. I did not know that I loved her – perhaps I did not love her – until one afternoon when I was lying down in the room I shared with my school friend, and Lana came to talk to me. It was a warm day in late April or early May. She sat on the bed and we talked for a long time, and I told her about my family and our country house, and slowly became aware that she was staring at me, and something in her regard made me falter and fall silent ... The last word I said, grotesquely unsuitable, was 'lepers', I remember: I had been describing how my mother knew about a leper colony somewhere near London. Lana smiled oddly at me, and said softly 'Go on – Lepers – ' and then slowly leaned across and kissed me on the mouth.

I was swept into a wild confusion of ecstasy and shyness;

I clasped her in my arms and she kissed me again and again. I had no idea of what had happened; my blood burned me, my heart-beat stifled me; I felt as though something had exploded beside me and I had been blown to atoms –

I remember that I stammered out a desperate question, 'What is it?' And Lana said 'I am in love with you, my darling – ' and I don't remember anything more until – perhaps hours later – she said we must go down to tea, and laughed because soon we should be in company and pretending to be only casual acquaintances, and would have to ask each other 'Milk, please – ' or 'Can I have the butter?'

We went down to tea (I was shaking so that I could scarcely walk) and then, across the table, Lana said to me 'Can I have the butter?' and I flushed and pushed it across so rudely that I was reprimanded by whichever of the ladies was superintending us that day.

After this, so far as we could manage to be, we were inseparable. Notes passed, and presents; we walked together; we sat together at the Opéra and at concerts. At last the day came when my sister and mother were arriving to stay a few days and I was to go to the Hotel Roosevelt, Avenue Roosevelt, to stay with them. I could scarcely bear to go; but then, waiting for them to arrive, I changed into my new evening dress and painted my lips as I had been taught, and sat – with my waved hair and made-up face – to wait for them in the lounge of the hotel. They arrived and stood there for some time and then walked past me and never recognized me at all. It was a moment of great triumph and happiness. I was, I thought, really 'out' at last. My sister could never catch me again. (That was not true.)

The days of their stay dragged, because I did not see Lana alone. We took her out to tea once, and once they visited Rue Ybry with me. And on that occasion Lana told me that she had arranged to change bedrooms; hitherto she had slept alone and I had shared my room; now she was to replace my school friend, who wanted to go upstairs to share a room with another young woman, a rich, sophisticated, noisy, vulgar young woman too.

'I shall have you to myself every night – ' said Lana, and I shook with fear and excitement and could not sleep that night and dared not think about how it would be.

On May 29th I returned to Rue Ybry; the room was full of flowers that Lana had bought; white lilac and white irises; a huge bunch of small rosebuds. She had got a screen too, so that we might dress and undress without being shy. Without this I could not have endured my extreme timidity.

That night I went upstairs first and Lana followed when I was in bed. We were both totally ignorant (innocent is the better word) and all we knew of love-making was to lie close together and kiss; but no two have ever loved more or been more completely, passionately fulfilled.

It was a very brief happiness; in the middle of June we left Paris and returned to England. My parents did not like Lana very much, and her home in one of the Kentish suburbs of London was like nothing I had ever seen before. Her mother was a commanding, stout, over-dressed woman, of infinitely kind heart and ferocious temper; her father drank too much and liked to tell stories about seeing girls' legs in railway carriages; there was a lean, spectacled man whom Lana called 'godfather', who was her mother's lover; he was clever and in some kind of wholesale dress business with her mother – he was a typical bourgeois businessman and, with less good fortune, he would have been the chief clerk in some solicitor's office. I liked none of them and they all thought my shyness and strangeness was 'side'. Beside Lana and her mother I felt very dowdy and poor, for they had luxurious satin underclothes and Lana had astonished me by the marvellous splendours of her printed silk pyjamas and the care she took about making-up, about hair-dressing, nail-varnishing, and the fact that directly she awoke in the morning, before her eyes were properly opened on the world, she sprang out of bed and sat down in front of her mirror, licking her forefinger and rubbing her eyebrows because 'Peggy' her mother 'made me promise always to do that; my eyebrows won't keep a good shape otherwise – '

Lana was typically suburban, typical flippant and silly, but these qualities went with others not so commonplace; she read a great deal and introduced me to many poems I had not heard of – she showed me the way to many things that now are the most precious I have. And she was sensitive, full of delicacy, full or amorousness and subtlety. She made love with an exquisite fervour and abandon and, for that brief time, we loved each other with truth and candour. It was like Daphnis and Chloe. It was classical and had no stain upon it.

That summer I spent in Norfolk and then, in September or October, Lana's mother asked me to go with them on a motoring tour abroad, and after some argument my parents consented – if I would first go to a Hunt Ball in Flintshire – or somewhere like that. I travelled to Symond's Yat with a tall American who was sent with me. I did not like him at all. He was extremely successful and handsome and he must have found me troublesome, for I had no idea of amusing him. I carried letters from Lana and her photograph and thought only of how I would soon see her again.

The Hunt Ball was dreadful. The Great Family was called Scudamore Stanhope and my host and hostess were anxious to prove that they were on familiar terms with the noblemen. I had to dance with a drunk young man, one of the S.S.s, who pulled off my slipper and mumbled my foot, I remember, and I had an embarrassing few moments before I could get him up on his feet again. I returned to my hostess's mother, a nice old lady, and steadily refused to dance with anyone again. Most people got drunk, which was then a strange and unaccustomed sight (I expect it has always happened at Hunt Balls but I had never met the genuine backwoods County before, and the sight appalled me). After a gruesome finale, when they all danced a gallop and many couples fell down flat on the floor, and the place resounded with cat-calls, yells, hunting-horns and a variety of horrible noises, we all returned home. It was about four in the morning, and at nine the American and I caught our train for London. He had been delighted by the company and felt still elated and we had a tiresome journey.

I was then only sixteen; I had weathered my first and last Hunt Ball, and now I was on the way to Europe again, and to Lana.

We crossed the Channel, and at St Omer the Studebaker car broke down. We stayed there for two or three days and then went on, through the battlefields of Flanders (still not tidied up – it was 1922 – and so oppressive to the spirit that I even lost any sense of joy in Lana's presence, and could not speak and could not endure to look at any of the

78

people I was with) and went on, over the Simplon, into Italy. We went to the Lakes, to Milan, to Turin, back to Switzerland, to Grindelwald, where Lana's mother and her godfather had to return by train to England for some emergency, and Lana and I were left alone, at the Bear Hotel, in great state, for five wonderful days. Then the others returned and we drove at a leisurely pace through France (we stayed a night at Annecy) and to Paris.

There, at the Hotel Continental, Lana's mother grieved because my clothes were so unsuitable to the splendour around us. She tried to persuade me to let her fit me out, but I would not because I was shy and proud and it seemed to me that to do so would be disloyal to my parents. I had a very childish sense of right and wrong – maybe it is truer to call it a sense of 'done' and 'not done'.

At last we returned home. All the journey we had shared a room, Lana and I, and Peggy had often referred to us as 'quite like lovers'. She was very kind to me, even when she must have been ashamed of me. I grew to respect and like her.

Meanwhile, at home, my sister (engaged but not yet married) had been reading letters from my desk and had, of course, easily discovered the situation between Lana and me. She told my mother, who tried to hush it up. But at length it got to my father and directly I was home he informed me that I was to be sent to a Domestic Training College at Eastbourne. I did not know why. I was horrified. For a year I had been to dances, opera, concerts; I had evening clothes; I thought of myself as grown up. Now I was to go back to school – worse, to a boarding-school: worst of all, to learn Domestic Economy, which seemed liked the lowest degradation to me. I begged to be allowed to take up music again, to have a tutor, to do *anything*; but he would not listen. On the morning of the day we were to leave for Eastbourne, he and my mother and I, my father came into my room as I was packing and began to question me, severely and furiously, about my relationship with Lana. I did not understand at all what he was trying to find out. I told him that we were in love.

I remember very vividly the expression of disgust on his face.

He became very angry indeed – much angrier than I had ever seen him before. He asked if I knew what a filthy thing I had been doing? I answered, No, it had not been at all filthy. It was something very strange, but not at all wrong. I thought one or other of us must have been wrongly made – He asked furiously what I meant? I said that Lana ought to have been a man; I thought she must have been one in a previous incarnation – He muttered something and rushed out of the room. My mother came in and began to question me more gently. I patiently explained that we had fallen in love; no one could help that, could they? It was wonderful. We were very, very happy. We would love each other for ever. What could be wrong in that?

They told me that the train went in half an hour and that Lana had confessed everything and her family were furious. I must not see her nor write to her ever again. I fought back then – and insisted upon telephoning her at once. I did so, and heard her in bitter tears, saying the same thing: we must not meet or write again. I had such complete confidence and trust in her that I never for a moment doubted but that she had been forced to this by her mother's rage. I assured her that I would be constant and not give way for a moment. She wept and reiterated that she had promised – we must never meet or write again. And then I was torn away and bundled into the Pullman coach of the Eastbourne express, where I sat facing my father – his face pale and set into lines of extraordinary anger. And at last we arrived.

We went to the Grand Hotel and my father came straight into my room and began to question me. He asked me if I realized that what Lana and I had done was the worst, filthiest (a word reiterated constantly, shocking me each time afresh), the most unforgivable thing that anyone could do? No decent man would marry me if he knew of it. My father was so horrified he could scarcely endure to see me. And so on. Then he used the word 'unnatural' – and I began to argue.

How could it be 'unnatural' when neither Lana nor I had any idea of it until we fell in love? We had not done anything wrong, I said; we had only loved each other –

It went on and on until my nerve broke and I wept. Then my mother came in and begged my father to leave me, and took me into her room and talked to me; but I stubbornly refused to admit that anything we had done *could* have been unnatural. How – if it was – had we done it? No one had ever told us anything –

All of these arguments, of course, convinced my parents that we had, in fact, been lovers in their *News of the World* sense of that word. Whereas, all the time, we had been as innocent as Daphnis and Chloe; more innocent, in one sense, because we had never known a moment's uneasiness or wonder or curiosity: we had been wholly satisfied to kiss and fondle and lie in bed close to each other and talk and laugh and be happy. My parents never did believe this, and for a full year I had no idea of their theories – I never moved from my position of absolute conviction that what we had done was right, inevitable and in the circumstances perfectly natural. My father never forgave me. My mother grieved for me and after his death accepted the whole position with a kind of generous shrewdness – adapting herself to the inevitable so as not to lose me, for she loved me very much.

At the College I was completely miserable. All the students were inimical to me and I to them. No one of my own class was there; no one with any interest in literature or painting or music. The place was (by an ironical stroke on the part of God) given over to unnatural vice. The headmistress was a pious, emotional, 'manly' bitch and the rest of the staff, with one exception, were delighted to encourage 'crushes' and 'pashes' and all the rest – At night, after lights out, the house used to echo and re-echo; doors slamming, footsteps, whispers, giggles – I had notes and posies left in my room and vile ogling advances made, and nudges and jokes and taunts. I had an attic room, to which I went whenever I could; I never would go near the Common Room, nor go out with any of the others into the town. At last, I suppose because of reports that I was pining, for I would not eat, my parents did the oddest thing: they sent Lana down to stay for one night and two days with me.

This was a tragic, a heartbroken meeting and parting. Lana told me that her parents had said to her what mine had said to me; but she had believed them. She *must* marry, she said; she *must* find someone who would marry her – Her mother had told her that unless she married she would be an old maid, disgraced, poor and unwanted. She wept; she lay in my bed and we talked till the day came, and then we wandered through the dismal streets, through a long, cold, autumn Sunday in that dreariest of all seaside towns, and then she went away.

After a few more weeks I was taken away and sent down to Sussex, to stay on a farm with some cousins. There I lived rough and among people who despised all the things I revered; but I had the care of two very handsome polo ponies, of the Argentine polo team, who were boarded there for the winter; these were a delight to me and for a while I and my misery managed to keep alive on the pleasure of having those creatures to ride and handle. But at last it was too much and I ran away. To do this I had to steal some money, for I had none; so I took my aunt's purse and bought a ticket to London and arrived at my parents' flat. They lived, then, in a service flat in a luxurious block in Westminster.

I do not remember the arrival. I remember the letter that came next day, saying that I had stolen this money, and the trouble about that. But by then I was so sick with misery and a kind of deadly, lonely despair, that I cannot remember anything in detail, except that I committed every kind of crime and offence; stealing, lying, romancing, falling into agonies of lust, without any idea of what I lusted for; and I could not seem to speak bare truth, even about the smallest things. I was always caught out; I made little or no attempt to cover my tracks. I read feverishly, all the poems I could get – I went to the forever-blessed Poetry Bookshop and bought cheap Broadsheets to hang on my walls, and learned the poems by heart; I sat for hours at a time, imagining the wildest dramas and being sometimes the heroine and sometimes the hero of them, but most often, I think, the heroine.

Among the dire results of my 'unnaturalness' I had been told that I should go blind and go mad. I believed this. In a kind of cold reasonableness, I tried to teach myself to type and play the piano with my eyes shut, against the time I should be blind. But the madness I could not think how to prepare for; and yet it seemed always more sure to come. I knew that everything I did was done without my will. I knew that I could not tell the truth, I could not refrain from buying what I wanted, and I could not control my wants; the oddest things seized upon my imagination.

I remember, for instance, that I saw in a cheapjack shop in Charing Cross road, an imitation gold half-hunter watch, a man's watch; it cost 10s. (London was full of stores that sold such things just then). I bought it, after agonizing for two days with longing for it. I stole the money to buy it, for I had only 10s. a week, and fares, gloves, stockings, hairdressing and all etc. had to come out of that. I don't remember how I stole the money. The watch, of course, was immediately noticed and my sister enquired where it had come from. I said that I had known a certain major – for some time now. He was in love with me, I said, and could not marry me because he was married already. Now he had gone abroad for ever, and left me this watch of his as a memento.

That odd, pathetic story caused the utmost consternation. My mother believed it and my sister, as she told me, 'made enquiries'. I grew alarmed, aware of the utter futility of the romance, and told them the truth. They did not believe the truth, but spent a long time hunting about to discover, if possible, *some* clue to this strange and wicked man ... And I was so sick, so miserable, so nearly mad that I lost all interest in the whole thing, and to this day I cannot tell what happened to the watch, nor how the story came to an end.

Family confusions added to everything else. My mother and father were unhappy together and my father tried to console himself for his great horror of me (he had loved me

84

very much) by cleaving to my sister and by going off for holidays to France with a disreputable grand friend of his and the friend's mistress. My mother disapproved of those people and there were frequent arguments and miseries.

My sister married, in the April, I think of that year, and my father disliked her husband, and she came to dislike him very soon afterwards. In August of that year my father died, suddenly and most shockingly, of cancer. In September my mother's brother-in-law died suddenly from a heart-attack. In the February her other brother-in-law died. These deaths frightened us all and made all our miseries worse, not better. My sister and my brother-in-law took command of our household for a while and made my life unutterably miserable.

I had been in touch with the young man I had been 'engaged' to when he was a schoolboy; at this period he was a planter in Java. One of my letters, after my father's death, was so unhappy that he cabled me to marry him and I cabled back that I would. We had not met since I was eleven or so.

The engagement was announced and presents began to come in. A trousseau was bought, and for a while I was very happy, getting ready and writing and receiving long letters. I would escape from my sister; I would be married; I would be away from everything that had been so nightmarishly miserable; I would have children – I longed passionately for children – And in the spring of the following year, 1924, I went with my mother to Switzerland for the last journey abroad before we sailed for Singapore.

On our return (we were not to sail until June) I had nothing to do and I took up political canvassing, and at that job I met a young woman speaker for the Conservative Party, who was extremely popular and attractive. She showed me great favour. She was twenty-eight at that time, which seemed to me extremely old (I was eighteen). One day she told me that she knew two dear old women, one French and the other English, who lived in Camberwell and kept a lodging house; the Frenchwoman was a marvellous cook. She would love to take me there to stay a night and eat a fine dinner – it would be an adventure, to stay in Camberwell, and fun, wouldn't it?

I was deeply flattered and we went.

That night, as we sat in our dressing-gowns by the fire in her bedroom, she took my hand and later, as I had got up to go to my room, she kissed me.

So it had happened again, and this time not to me innocent but to me sullied by reproaches and arguments and misapprehensions, but as ignorant as ever; for I knew nothing about lesbianism, except that now I knew it existed and was, instead of being something that had miraculously happened to me alone, something almost commonplace, and something that aroused loathing and vituperation.

In the morning, I remember, she woke me in my bed, for after we had talked a little about how we had fallen in love, I had gone back to my room. My first words to her, spoken to give me courage, I fancy, and to show her that I was sophisticated and 'hard', were 'Well, I suppose it is all over?' And she replied, 'No – this is only the beginning of the beginning – '

And so it was.

We were lovers from 1924 until 1930, and in that period I broke one engagement, and married, and left my husband, and fell in love many times, but still she and I remained lovers and again and again I returned to her, until at last I fell in love for life.

[IV]

I have now weaned myself (have I?) from the lusts of the flesh; from the amorous lusts, anyhow. I live chastely, do I? But would I? It is true that I have sailed my boat around an unnamed Cape, after travelling the fierce, open seas, over the dangerous shoals of those ages thirty-three, thirty-four, thirty-five, and on to forty itself; ages that came near to wrecking me, boat and all (and often I felt as though I had no boat beneath me, but at best a breaking raft, a spar, and my own half-frozen limbs to carry me).

Then, at forty-one or so, I found myself in calm water, near to a curve of new coast-line, unexplored; and looking, as land does from the sea, marvellously enticing and tidy and full of promise. But am I secure? The merest breath from the shore, a nostalgic breath of roses and wood smoke, and what would then happen to me?

Still, it has sobered me to learn what a wreck can be made; and now I know what one rebuilds, with infinite pains, from the splinters and wreckage, is not the same ship. Perhaps it is more seaworthy, but the lines are not as beautiful, the curves not as harmonious, and it is not the original, the first, the proudest.

It goes against my secret pride (and the secret intention, that everyone has, to excel in living a life) to admit that I owe everything to another person. But if she had not had an extraordinary (and mainly a deliberately made) character, an intellect and spirit full of power and courage, we would have been wrecked and ruined together because of my folly, because of my privy shame.

In 1923, before I fell in love this second time, my father died, as I have said. I was in the midst of my half-crazy folly then, and the grief I felt, and the fear and shuddering sensation of shock that came upon me because he had died, were sometimes less real than my fancies, and sometimes so much more real that I could scarcely bear to know myself at all.

In that year I was really 'out'. In May of the year I had given a coming-out dance, and now my mother's insistence that death was nothing to care a straw about gave us a licence to live in a riot of dances and parties; more than licence – it forced upon us (upon me at any rate) a strange desperation of enjoyment – as though I owed it to her as a duty to be as reckless and assertive as I could manage. That is how it seemed sometimes, at least. And the period favoured it. London was extremely gay, and it was fashionable to commit extravagancies and follies. I remember wearing a bare-backed, sleeveless bright green evening dress and screwing a horn-rimmed monocle into my eye, and walking down the steps into the Savoy Ballroom like that – at the age of seventeen – for a bet. And a fine image of folly I made myself, and desperately shy and ashamed I was of the stir I caused, too. And after all, it ended in paying 10s. 6d. for the right to dance there for three or four hours, and to drink orangeade at 2s. 6d. a time with the young man of twenty who was my partner for the evening. an unsophisticated young man, if ever there was one; who was delighted and a little afraid to be out with such a smart devil-may-care young woman. And so we drank our orangeade and chattered, as best we might, in imitation of the Bright Young People of that date. And I think we enjoyed it quite fairly, and I know that we enjoyed the act of dancing more than anything else, because we had the skill for it. But we had no emotion whatever towards each other, and indeed, at that date, I had not experienced any physical emotion for any young man, nor responded at all to the few who seemed to be excited by me. And I could not tell in the least if they really were, but always suspected that they were not, for I had no assurance at all, nor any belief in myself, and most things seemed dreamlike and unreal, unless I remembered Lana – and then my heart bled slowly and painfully until all my strength drained away.

Lana, meanwhile, had become engaged to her cousin, a fat young man who drank too much. He was singularly unappetizing and very boastful; I believed then that she loved him and yet I also believed that she loved me.

My sister persuaded my mother that I must be made to go to the wedding, and I was so made. It was a wedding above their station – indeed, they tried very hard to be married at St Margaret's, Westminster, but this could not be managed; so they had the service at St Peter's, Eaton Square, which was at that time the church that the more dubious of the rich patronized. I can remember the ceremony vaguely; all the time I was absorbed in the strange sensation of inward bleeding, and I felt faint and very weak, as though I were in fact bleeding inwardly. There was a reception at the Hyde Park Hotel, and a newspaper peer made a speech (he was the father of the bridegroom by a woman writer of crime stories, and this was considered to be in the young man's favour, by most of the guests, but my mother disapproved). The peer was drunk, and he made a lecherous speech and ended by holding Lana to his breast and kissing her very passionately.

I stood beside the long table, crowded with food and glasses, and tried to realize that that small, flushed face and those bright eyes belonged to my love, but I realized nothing except that I felt very ill and that if I were to regain full consciousness I should find myself in intolerable pain.

But I did not regain consciousness; not even when I had to visit Lana in her little pretty Georgian house in Catherine Street. We sat in the sitting-room and talked like two young women who had been school friends, and then I went away. I have never seen her since.

As 1923 ended, 1924 brought its new love. And for a while it went smoothly, and I was profoundly happy, profoundly disturbed.

I went to Spain early in 1925 with the young woman and her brother, a loutish officer in the army. My grandmother had died and left me £50, and on that somehow I managed to go with them to Spain. On the liner going to Gibraltar, on the first night aboard, the young woman (whom we will call X) made love to me. Now I was not innocent any more; I knew little or nothing about how to make love, but I had a passionate desire to know, and I did not realize that she was cautious, and indeed that she was considerate and gentle with me. I was happier that I had ever been, I suppose, but now not without misgivings, not without a feeling of secret triumph, a sense that what I was doing, what was being done to me, was wicked, dangerous, marvellously daring.

X was a Roman Catholic. It had taken me only a few months to be converted. I was already having Instruction from a priest, and I was quite untroubled by scruples, quite serenely confident that what we were doing was

90

legitimate, while at the same time I relished the fact that it was extremely sinful and secret.

X conjured me to be very cautious and never to let anyone suspect we were lovers. I did ask her what I should do about Confession when I had been received into the Faith, and she replied that she never troubled in the least about it; what we were to each other was perfectly all right; we were in love; God could not mind that; indeed, she said, he could only approve it, so long as what we did caused no damage to anyone else. I accepted this, knowing, in some cold corner of my mind, that it was casuistry, and perhaps liking it the better for that – or taking pleasure in the intellectual twists of my own mind as I accepted it.

On board that ship a Frenchwoman, a small brilliant creature with shining green-glass eyes, asked me about my engagement ring. I told her about going out to Java. It was now February, and I was due to sail in June. She smiled and wagged her head at me and told me I should never go. 'You are not for that young man!' she said and laughed. I felt at once elated and depressed.

On the way home I grew sad and decided that I could not possibly leave X. What should I do? She had no counsel to offer. If her parents died, she said, then we would go to live together in a cottage in the country and love and be happy. But until they died she must stay with them – time would show, she said, what we could do, and meanwhile, were we not very happy?

Yes, yes, we were – I said – but I wept when I parted from her at the station, and went back to my mother, to the heap of letters from Java, the wedding presents, the sailing tickets.

And then (how many things crowd into a year when one

is so young!) one day I went to visit a cousin of mine in a nursing-home, and in his room met a tall young man with hair so golden that it looked almost green. He was shy and very nice to me.

Two weeks later I went to Liverpool Street Station to meet my mother, returning from a weekend in Norfolk, and met the young man again. He had been staying nearby. He attached himself to me, shyly but persistently. My mother asked him to dinner a few nights later.

It was a small dinner-party, and we were the only young people there. After dinner we talked for a long time together and I told him about becoming a Catholic, and in a trice persuaded him that he should.

Next day, as I was having tea alone in the flat, in he walked, and announced that he had something to say to me. I looked up at him and thought he looked very handsome; and he had a shy but positive manner which pleased me. He was, too, the first young man interested in music and writing, anxious to argue and discuss, who had fallen in love with me. The four or five others from whom I had had what this one called 'sacred or profane proposals' were all *nice normal people*, as my mother said. Richard stood beside me as I thought of all this, and then I looked up and said 'All right; I am engaged already, and going to Java in three months. But I'll marry you at once, if you want me to.'

Richard sat down promptly, taking my hand in an absent-minded way, and beginning to question me about my engagement. He had not noticed my ring, he said; but if I had thought of going to Java that really was serious – of course I must marry him at once, or else I would be lost for ever. Lost to him, he added, for no doubt I would be very happy if I went to Java.

This kind of lukewarm, slightly disjointed courtship gave me great pleasure. It suited the almost total unreality of my state of mind and emotions. I do not remember thinking of X at all, although with her, and only with her, I was freed into reality and lived as if I were in my wits. But I thought of the man in Java, and felt worried to know which I really wanted to do. I did not think of him or of Richard; I thought of what I wanted to do, and even that only hazily. Perhaps because my body was wholly given over to X, whose love excited and satisfied me, profoundly and superficially too, I did not even think whether I felt desire towards Richard. But the situation was amusing; it was modern and emancipated; and Richard was a little intimidating when he looked at me; I was shy of him, anxious to impress him, anxious not to annoy him, anxious – above all – to appear sophisticated and competent to deal with this or any other situation.

I said, 'But do you love me?'

He said, 'I suppose I do. I have thought of no one else since last night; and before last night, after seeing you at the station, I walked about in a dream and you were the dream.'

I was entranced by this: I said, 'I am afraid I love you, too,' and Richard then got up and said, 'We ought to kiss, then. Will you marry me?'

And I got up, and said very formally, 'Yes, I will marry you,' and as Richard kissed me (very violently, to my astonishment and distaste) my mother came into the room.

If she had not come in just then, I am almost sure that I would have changed my mind once for all. I definitely did not like being kissed by Richard. But my mother exclaimed, grew very pale, rushed across the room and

93

cried out dramatically, 'What is all this? *What* – ' And Richard, also growing very pale but looking extremely handsome and carrying the situation with great dash, replied, 'Your daughter is going to marry me. I hope you don't mind?'

My mother sat down and stared at us; then she turned on me and said sharply, 'But you are engaged. How dare you do this?'

And I, entranced by the developments of the situation and delighted at the quick, dramatic movement of events, answered meekly, as I thought befitted me, 'I am sorry – I could not help it. I have fallen in love with Richard.'

My mother groaned, but in her groan I detected the same enjoyment that I was feeling. She turned her attention to Richard and told him about my engagement, about our projected journey to Java, about the wedding presents, the trousseaux, the tickets for the steamer, the two Siamese cats I had bought to take with me ...

And Richard laughed and said, 'I'm very sorry. It is all very awkward. But we can't do anything about it. I am sorry for the man in Java. But she is going to marry me.'

My mother wavered; she obviously liked Richard; and indeed, he carried the situation charmingly, looking embarrassed but determined and glancing from one to the other of us with eyes which, then, seemed bright and large, though in fact they were rather small and unusually unsure and without any brightness.

It was agreed, at last, that he should go away and not see me, nor write to me for some time – an unspecified time – at least until I had written to the man in Java, and my mother had thought things over.

'May I write to you, to keep in touch?' demanded Richard.

94

'Yes,' she said, and smiled.

'Then good-bye for a little while,' he said, taking my hand and bending over me. I avoided his lips and he kissed my hair. Then, as he went to the door, I said 'Give me your address. I don't know where you live – '

And he took out a visiting-card and gave it to me, and went away.

'I think you are quite mad – ' said my mother, and nothing could have delighted me more.

It was evening by then, but my mother and I sat and talked, in a musing way, quite amicably; obviously we both of us felt relaxed and happy, delighted as though we had been out at a party. At about seven a messenger-boy arrived with a huge box of flowers addressed to my mother and sent by Richard. Next morning a box containing the recordings of *Til Eulenspiegel*, by Richard Strauss, arrived, and with them a visiting-card saying, 'To Mrs —— from Richard ——'. And then a long letter to her, praising me, and ending 'O Shenandoah, kind regards to your daughter – '

While this oblique courtship continued I was very happy; but I do not remember that I told X anything much about it. I wrote to Java, and this letter was easier because I had just received one telling me that if I became a Catholic, I could not engage to bring up my children as Catholics; otherwise, he hinted, he would not marry me. For a moment this pleased me; I wrote a long letter, explaining to my own satisfaction what had happened, and when his reply came, full of bewilderment and reproach, I did not feel at all guilty. But later, for some reason, I felt uncomfortable because he had been shocked at my becoming a Catholic; I felt as if I had lost something – almost as if I had disgraced myself.

I wonder if anyone in the world was ever so idiotically vile as I was, for the best part of my youth.

And all the time X was making love to me and writing to me, and in everything she said in praise of me some words appeared continually, grotesquely inappropriate to the person I have been accurately describing: the words were 'fastidiously discriminating' and 'your sensitive intelligence'.

Did I believe them? I believed everything that was told me of myself; I believed them; and I believed my sister when she told me I was a degenerate, a hopeless case, practically an idiot; and I believed a young man who told me I was without any heart and intent only upon breaking other people's hearts; and I believed an eccentric, drunken doctor who – years before – had told me that I had an erratic, creative spirit allied to a good brain, and God only knew what that would lead to; and I believed a fat young man who told me that I was an uneducated little bourgeois, doomed to be a perpetual virgin. I believed everyone's assessment of me, good and bad, but the good misled me and the bad horrified me, and if anyone had talked to me soberly and told me that in ten years' time I should be changing, and in twenty years I should be unrecognizable, I would have been at first comforted and then I would not have been able to believe it: for I never could believe that anything would be *all right*. I believed it would be marvellous, or unbearably dreadful, but *all right*; safe; gentle; serene: I never believed that, even when I most nearly believed in God.

1925 was a curious year. I have had to reckon out the dates of all the things that happened then, and it is hard to believe that so much could be squeezed in to so little time. But days were infinitely long, and charged with emotion, with all kinds of wild, extravagant situations. At first it is impossible to see any continuity in what actually happened from day to day; but when I stare hard enough I see my small square bedroom, and the fragile satinwood desk in which I kept my poems, and the wall, decorated with two or three broadsheets ('There is a lady sweet and kind,' 'Men when their affairs require,' 'Never seek to tell thy love' –) and several postcards on which I had typed out poems I liked: Raleigh's 'Even such is time/That takes in trust' and Wyatt's 'Forget Not Yet,' Verlaine's 'Les sanglots longs/des violons ... ' and 'Dans le vieux parc solitaire et glacé'. All these I read and re-read, as I dressed, as I did my hair, as I moved about my room. And I experienced a deep and shaking ecstasy when I read a poem – when I read Keats's 'Ode to Melancholy' – when I read in a whisper to myself line on line of Shakespeare. I wrote feverishly; into the night I wrote, I wrote all day; I wrote in buses and in the lavatory; I wrote in the cloakrooms of restaurants, of hotels where I had gone out to dance; I wrote abject nonsense, which sickened me because it was so revoltingly sentimental and unlike the *thing I had in my head*. And during the time I was under Instruction, and went to the Clergy House at Westminster Cathedral three times a week, I wrote sometimes poems about God, strictly theological poems, and sometimes angry poems against God ... None of either sort were ever in the least like the thought (or the notion) in my head. But whenever I prayed (and I prayed fervently and long, with desperate pleadings) I always found myself confronted with a stern uncompromising choice: either this (whatever I so feverishly wanted at the moment) or poetry; not both. And I always, in fear and often in despair but always unhesitatingly, chose poetry ... Whatever *that* was: for I

97

never dared believe I'd get it. (And 'get' what?)

From X I learnt a great deal besides how to make love, and that too I learned very well. She introduced me to books, to modern pictures, to modern poetry. And my sister, too, had introduced me to this last: I owed her the Poetry Bookshop, for one thing; and I owed to her a restless determination to reject everything that had been to my parents' liking: plays, songs, music, pictures, fashions, 'taste'. They were 'middle-class', my sister said, and by implication we were not. To my sister, too, I owe knowledge of Anatole France: and at that time an English edition of his works was coming out, at half-a-crown a volume, and I used to go to the Army and Navy Stores and buy them as they came – I have them all now, and they are very dear to me. I do not know how I managed to buy them all, for as I was in love now I never had any money.

After a short while my mother relented and Richard was allowed to visit me. I almost at once ceased to love him, and would not agree to marry. I did, very sensibly, suggest that we should go abroad together and 'try it out' but he would not agree, and of course my mother would not. Richard argued that as to-be-Catholics (he was taking Instruction too) we could not deliberately commit that sin. I knew that he was right, and I knew also that he was wrong. However, my mind was set on X still, and the rare occasions that we could spend a night together swept all thought of Richard out of my head. We never, at this time, did more than embrace and caress; but the least contact with her made me completely happy, full of delight, tossed into ecstasy. I wanted nothing more than her least caress, and to be with her, and she seemed to be completely satisfied with this. She wrote to me every day, and I to her; she gave me countless presents; although by now she knew

98

about Richard, and even came out with us, she did not appear to be perturbed, and this distressed me sometimes; but in my odd state of mind it did not worry me for long.

However, I *was* unsettled, and so, of course, was Richard. And in early May of that same year – when I was in Paris with my mother – he arrived at our hotel unexpectedly, and demanded that my mother should make me go out with him that evening; and she told me that I must, and although I was reluctant, I did. We went to a music hall and saw Mistinguette; we drove through Paris in an open taxi, seeing other pairs of people, usually making love. Suddenly I felt that it was all clear, simple, straightforward: of course I loved Richard. All the rest was dream, folly, and might become madness! I would cast it off once for all; I would marry him, I would become, once for all, just like all these other people! I threw myself into his arms and, for a brief half-hour or so, I felt enchanted – it was all clear and easy and nothing else mattered. So we were engaged again, and the next day Richard returned to London, and after two days or so my mother and I returned too.

Richard sent me telegrams two or three times a day, while we were still in Paris, and he met us at Victoria. I did not like him when I saw him again; for the first time I noticed that he looked – as it were – *meagre*. Next morning X telephoned me, and when I heard her voice I wept.

So it went on until early June, and then one day I had a sharp quarrel with my mother; it was only one of many, for we loathed each other then; and in the middle of it my sister appeared and took me aside and began to reason with me. She told me that I *must* marry; never mind who – Richard as well as anyone else. I could not otherwise escape from my mother; I should be one of those miserable, dowdy daughters, travelling from place to place, unhappy, cheated, oppressed. Even if I did not think I loved Richard – or anyone else – I must at least *marry*. Once that was done, she assured me, things would get better. Even if I did not love my husband (and probably I would) then at least I should be free from Home. Look at her, she said – she was free.

I was interested by the implication that she was not in love with her husband. It did not surprise me nor shock me, but I saw in it an odd kind of reassurance: as if nothing was nearly as difficult and dangerous as I thought it. Just get married – and everything was all right.

I rang up Richard and asked him to meet me for lunch. We went to a restaurant in the Strand and I said 'I will marry you if you will marry me tomorrow. I won't if it is put off for a day.'

Richard protested that I had never even seen his parents; they knew nothing about me; it wasn't fair to them – How could he depend on me, either? I had promised him twice, and twice broken it off.

Yes, I said, and so I shall again unless we do it tomorrow.

He looked at me sadly, and then suddenly he said all right. But he must tell his mother, for he loved her. She was down at Coombe Martin, near Ilfracombe, he said; how could he see her and marry me next day?

Opposition excited me and I was resolved to have my way. He could get the licence; I would make the appointment with the registrar, I said; he could catch the evening train to Devonshire and I would travel down by car and pick him up at midnight by the Ilfracombe post office. We would drive back to London and be married next day before three in the afternoon (later than that, in those days, you could not be married).

He too was excited by now, and he paid the bill, got up, kissed my hand and vanished into the Strand, on his way to Somerset House to get a special licence. I returned to my mother and told her, and after a protest she too became infected with the excitement and the difficulties and agreed. I got the route from the AA and my mother got a hamper of food from Fortnum and Mason; we got into the little open Wolseley car she had then, and started for Ilfracombe.

It was a wonderful drive; I felt elated and delighted. Just before we started I had telephoned X and told her briefly what I was doing. She made no comment at all. This wounded me and I felt as though all that had been cleanly ended, and now I was going to be a different person – I had had my nineteenth birthday in May, and by the time I was twenty, I told myself, I should be married and probably pregnant. The idea enchanted me. I drove fast, and sang; my mother sat beside me; she seemed happy too. Our quarrel was forgotten. We felt very friendly together. It was a lovely evening. The sunset was long and brilliant, and when it became dark we lost the way temporarily and I ran the car into a ditch.

After many adventures, we reached Ilfracombe at midnight, and there was Richard. It was a cold night and there was no one else in the street. He came over to the car and said that he could not marry me; his parents had said it was a mad thing to do, and insisted that he should wait for a week at least, and they would come to London and see me.

I was furious; I felt that I could not return to London and just tamely settle down into an engagement. If I did not marry him within the next twelve hours or so, I never never would.

He urged that we were not yet Catholics; we should wait until we had been received into the Church. I answered that if we got married in a Registrar's Office, and did not lie together, the Church would hurry up about it, and take us in, for fear that we would sin – Richard had been getting impatient at the delay, for he was a fervent convert by now, and he liked this idea of blackmail. At last, after many arguments, he climbed into the car and we started for London. I had driven a long way and grew sleepy now, and Richard took the wheel. I put my head on his shoulder and went to sleep. At Devizes he stopped and we had breakfast, and he went off for a walk. Then we started again and reached London at about ten o'clock. Richard went to get shaved; I telephoned the school-friend who had been with me in Paris, to come as a witness, and at two o'clock we were married at the Westminster Registrar's Office.

As we came out a small crowd cheered us; we got into the car and drove back to the flat. We dined together, but we were tired out and it was a sombre dinner, and then Richard went off to his club to sleep and I to my own bed. In the morning I had a moment of pure joy when I looked at the gold ring on my finger and thought 'There! I've done it!'

[V]

I was still, you see, free from any *fixed* vice: I have never thought (do not now, and do not expect to think) homosexuality wrong; that it is still considered to be a social offence makes it dangerous to a certain type of mind – offences against Society often intoxicate the offender, and the righteous who condemn them very often become intoxicated too. But I am sure that the impulse of desire towards someone of the same sex is not in itself wrong: it is not an offence in any degree – neither against God nor Man. And although for a short time I took pleasure in thinking I was flouting Society, it was exactly the same degree of pleasure that I felt when I wore a daringly low-cut dress, or first wore trousers and walked in Mecklenburgh Square (in 1926 this was a startling thing to do), or did any one of the many defiant things people of my age were doing at that time. For the rest, I know now that I was quite normally neither over- nor under-sexed, and that if Richard had been anything but what he was we should have become reconciled to our state, and, for a time at any rate, we should have been happy.

But Richard was without any experience of women, and he was suffering from remorse and fear because of certain homosexual relationships he had enjoyed recently. 'Enjoyed' is the important word. He was now horrified to remember that he had been happy.

I was remarkably stupid. I believe I was not really much interested. At all events, I listened to what he had to tell me but without my attempt to understand, beyond the plain fact that he had been loved by a man, whom he introduced to me, and that he felt even now disturbed and unhappy when he met him again. I was surprised that I did not feel jealous, but I soon forgot all about it. Richard, after a few attempts to confide in me, stopped talking about it. He set himself to desire me, and I think perhaps he succeeded. But I was at this time completely indifferent. I think I was tired out by the emotional stresses of the past three years, and I was also wholly absorbed in my love for X, although I did not admit this at that time.

The interval between our civil and religious weddings was spent mainly in interviews with our religious Directors: both of whom were very angry with us. Mine, a disillusioned, cynical man, gave me a brief lecture and then set out to persuade the authorities to receive us into the Church immediately. Richard's, a Jesuit, was much angrier, but he, too, tacitly admitted that we had forced his hand. We were, separately, received into the Church, baptized, then together we were confirmed by Cardinal ——, and about eight days after our first wedding we were married at Westminster Cathedral.

The day before this I saw X who told me that she would not attend the marriage; she had stood sponsor for me at my christening, and she lent me a very handsome jewel to wear at my wedding (this seemed to me strange, and I did not at all want to wear it, but she insisted). My wedding-dress was the ordinary kind of thing, pretty and white, but for head-dress I insisted upon having a nun-like coif, and this was a strange sight at that time (it is commonplace now, but in those days, so far as I know, no one had worn such a thing). The wedding was at 9 a.m. and the reception was to be held at 2.30 or 3, with a luncheon-party before it. In the interval between breakfast and lunch I went off to the hairdresser and had my hair Eton-cropped. This I did out of defiance and because I wanted to shock and astonish people. I did not consult Richard beforehand, but he was delighted with the result (and possibly because it made me look extremely boyish ... I was very tall and thin at that time; standing at almost six-foot and weighing just under eight stone) and while I wore my bridal head-dress no one saw what I had done. When I changed into my 'going-away' outfit, I chose not to wear a hat, and I was gratified by the sensation I caused when I came down into the large *salon* ... an old lady came up to me and said violently 'I have never seen an Eton-cropped bride before, and I hope I never shall again – it is disgusting!' I do not know who she was. There were a great many people there whom I did not know; people who had been my father's patients, and people who knew Richard's parents, and people, I think, who had gate-crashed the reception. Press photographers took pictures, and I was disappointed when I found that only one paper, I think, showed me with my Eton-crop, and all the rest were the usual 'Bride's Novel Head-Dress' photographs.

Richard, during the week between the weddings, had been told that he must undergo an operation immediately; it was not serious but it had to be arranged that he should be operated on the morning after our wedding. I was perfectly content with this arrangement, except that I was sorry for Richard who, I thought, must be very frightened at the prospect of having an operation. I did not in the least mind that we should not sleep together that night. It astonished me that he and my mother decided that no one should know about this arrangement, and that we should drive off in a motor car as though we were going to a station to set out on the honeymoon. In fact, we drove into the Park and round the Park, and back to my mother's flat. (The reception had been held at St James's Court, but my mother's flat there was let, and we had been living in Hertford Street, Park Lane, during that summer.)

Back at the flat, on a lovely June afternoon, we did not know what to do. Richard kissed me once or twice but we were shy of each other. Eventually we went out for an early dinner and then drove to his nursing-home. I enjoyed being called 'Mrs' and enjoyed the interested glances of the nurses, and the matron's sympathetic assurances that he would be all right. I felt sorry for Richard, but I could see that he was not particularly worried and so we kissed and I went home to bed.

Next evening I was allowed to visit him, and I visited him twice each day for a week, and then he came out cured, and now we were to set out on a honeymoon. My mind misgave me now. It had been arranged that we were to go to my mother's Norfolk house; I felt embarrassed because of the servants, and I did not like the idea of sleeping with Richard in what I knew as the 'spare room'. One or two of the servants had come up to the wedding, but no one else had seen Richard, and I wondered what they would think of him. In the train, too, the guard and inspector knew us very well, and we were given a carriage to ourselves, and people came and congratulated us and grinned and made little jokes. I half-liked this. Richard looked pale but quite handsome and he had a nice suit, I remember, which I had chosen for him. But I did not like him to look at me and I hated to sit close to him, and his hands seemed too large and curiously insensitive. I was thinking about X all the time, and making comparisons, against my will – for I felt this was unfair to Richard, and not kind of me. I do not think I had any sensation of disgust at my duplicity.

I had seen X every day while Richard was in the nursing-home. She told me that now we must not be lovers any more, and I had agreed, feeling rather noble and resolute, and quite failing (or avoiding) to understand that every glance and word that passed between us was an expression of love. The day before I left for my honeymoon X wept bitterly; I left her with my heart almost broken. I went to a flower shop and arranged that during the fortnight of my absence roses should be sent to her every day – and I left a note for each day – and each note had words of love and faith and promise.

When we arrived at the house we had dinner, and then the evening dragged on. My maid was now to be the housekeeper of my mother's house, and she was there. She hated my marriage – there should be a great deal about her in this account and I must remember to write it, for she was my truest, my closest and best friend from the time Blossom left until the time she herself married. At this moment, then, she was in the house and in a state of stern sorrow, scarcely speaking to me, and avoiding any chance of being alone with me.

'Shall I help you to undress?' she asked. But I said No. I loved her deeply and I could see her anguish of mind; and I felt it, obscurely myself, and did not want her to know this.

Richard went off to have a bath and I went into what had been my bedroom for so many years. I undressed and put on my silk nightgown. Then, after my bath, as Richard was not yet out of his, I went along to the dining-room and did a very extraordinary thing, that I had never done before. I poured out a stiff brandy and soda and drank it off.

This made my head dizzy and made me feel much better. I went to clean my teeth and as I passed the bedroom door Richard called me. I did not reply.

I went along to say good-night to my maid, but we were both very much embarrassed and I felt more miserable still. Then I went into the spare bedroom.

There were two beds: Richard lay in one and when he saw me he smiled nervously and said 'It's a pity there are two beds. Shall I come into yours?'

'If you like,' I said oddly.

He got out of his bed and I looked at him and felt afraid. The brandy made me feel only half real, and I was thankful for that. He got into my bed and turned off the light. As he lay very close to me I felt the hairs on his arms and loathed him.

We did not accomplish anything that night. I was perfectly uncooperative and I do not think Richard felt more than an occasional impulse of desire.

A week went by, and I was still a virgin. Richard's attempts hurt me and I resisted him; this frightened him badly, and I scorned him for being frightened.

Another week went by similarly, and then my mother joined us. I did not tell her anything at all.

The summer dragged on; Richard and I were only occasionally happy in each other's company; most of the time we were frightened of each other. Then X came down to stay with us, and for some while she and I kept aloof from each other, but there – in that burning summer, in the place where we had so often made love, we gradually slipped back into the old ways, and at last we went out together and lay under a haystack in the bright sunshine and made love and were profoundly happy and deeply unhappy, too.

One day, I remember, when we had come back from bathing and were still undressed, Richard called me into our room and directly I appeared he pulled me down onto the bed and began to make love to me. I was suddenly excited and delighted and yielded to him gladly. But again, after much pleasure, he hurt me too much and I wept, and he desisted.

After this he talked seriously to me and said I must go to see a doctor; and we went to London, and both saw different doctors. I was told that my hymen was too tough and that I was very small, and it might be as well to have an operation. Richard was told that he must deflower me, or else he would inhibit himself and do himself a nervous injury. We were recommended to go away together completely alone, and we went to Oxford and stayed at the Golden Cross hotel; but there we were very unhappy indeed and nothing came of it.

At last we had to go back to London and Richard was due to start work in his father's office. We got a dismal flat in Bayswater, No. 32 Colville Terrace, and moved in. Then the real trouble started.

Every night was an anguish to both of us, for by then Richard had begun to desire me and I had decided that I could not love him at all. I invented excuses, I pretended illnesses, I tried to starve myself; and every day I met X, who lived nearby, and at last we became lovers again, and only once, that I remember, did it occur to me sharply that I was deliberately committing adultery. I told her this and she answered that if I really believed this I must not do it; but she, for her part, did not think it anything of the sort – I did remain honest inside my head, and yet decided that I would go on committing this sin, for I could not endure my life unless I had this love.

109

Now I was slipping into the habit of drinking; for every day I would not eat except the minimum of food, and every day I drank gin or some sort of spirit; and I smoked a great deal. When I was a little fuddled in my head I could just endure my life. I did not realize what I was doing –

X, in all innocence, had started me on this way. At our first dinner together, when I was seventeen, she had given me champagne and at all subsequent dinners we drank wine, and sometimes she gave me brandy or whisky; I felt released from shyness and timidity, when I was a little drunk, and I became amusing and beguiling. I knew – and as it were I became *integrated*, together in myself, and possessed myself. I thought that without it I should slip back into being afraid; and I knew instinctively that without that to make me unreal I should see myself as I was, and I dared not.

Confused and miserable and sickened by Richard's love-making I went off to see a woman doctor, who told me that I must have an operation before I could have intercourse, and that I was so very small that it would be considerably dangerous for me to have a child.

I asked my confessor what I should do, and he said that I must have the operation, and I must have a child. There was no question about it – danger or not – it was my duty to do everything that Richard asked of me.

I told Richard; and he agreed instantly. He would, he said, insist that I should lie with him, and he would do his best to get me with child. He wanted a child more than anything else. It was every Catholic's duty, in marriage, to get a child.

Now I was in a dilemma. I was physically afraid and I was physically revolted by Richard. But I was deeply concerned to do what I should do. I cannot explain this;

for I was knowingly committing a great sin, in having X as a lover, and I knew that I was committing many other sins, innumerable and weak and vile sins, every day; and yet I felt a pure desire to do well.

One day, very miserable – much more miserable than I can explain – I was walking in Soho Square, for some reason, and I saw the Catholic church of St Patrick. I went in and prayed. Suddenly I became possessed with the desire to make my confession and I went into the first box that was occupied. The priest listened and questioned me; I told him everything – about Richard, about X, about drink, about what the doctor had said. He was gentle and unsurprised; he gave me a light penance and told me to come and see him again, at the presbytery.

After a few days I did so, and he turned out to be a tall, young Irishman, with an exceedingly gentle, passionate face. He and I sat in a bleak sitting-room, on hard chairs, and he questioned me with great gentleness and under-standing. I again told him everything I could. He reflected and then told me that it was as I had been told before: I must submit to Richard in everything; I must, if God willed it, have a child; it was in God's hands if I lived or died. My first duty was to have the operation and give Richard every chance to enjoy his rights. I looked at him in despair as he told me this, and to my astonishment, and to my great consolation, his eyes filled with tears and he wept.

'I am sorry – I am sorry – ' he kept on saying to me, and then he told me that he was going to be moved, and could not be my confessor, although he would have wished to be; and then he dismissed me and promised to pray for me.

I went back and told Richard I would have the operation.

A few days later it was arranged and I went into a nursing-home.

Walter Savage Landor says, in a letter dated 1835,

Nothing affects me but pain and disappointment. Hannah More says, 'There are no evils in the world but sin and bile.' They fall upon me very unequally. I would give a good quantity of bile for a trifle of sin, and yet my philosophy would induce me to throw it aside ... Happy he, who is resolved to walk with Epicurus on his right and Epictetus on his left, and to shut his ears to every other voice along the road.

At this juncture of my life, if I had been capable of understanding my own heart, or if I had been fortunate enough to have read this letter (which would have sent me off on a search for Epicurus and for Epictetus, to my great profit) I should have recognized where truth lay: for 'my philosophy' – in the sense of my (instinctive) love of wisdom – 'would induce me to throw it aside ... '

That is difficult to believe, I suppose, for anyone who has followed my course so far. But it is true. If I was not actively tormented, I was all the time weighed down with the burden of my spirit's ill health. Lying in the nursing-home, terrified of having an operation, dreading pain, tortured by my own cowardice, I clung to the remembrance of X, clutched in my hand a little silver box she had sent to me, inscribed with the words 'lovynge deare', and trying to believe I could rely on her. But I knew I could not. And I could not rely on myself. And I could not rely on Richard. I got out of my bed and knelt down and prayed; but when they brought in the stretcher and wheeled me off along the passageways, all I could do was to behave as artificially as possible, giving such a show of intrepidity that they were all deceived, but I was not; and as I went under the anaesthetic I thought desperately, 'I can't rely on myself – '

The period in the home was difficult; I was almost happy, except that in my cowardice the dread of having dressings (which were done morning and evening) filled all the first few days. I discovered that the authorities were quite prepared for me not to see Richard. They did not seem to think it unusual that I should not want to. For three days or more I did not see him, and then when he came he was very angry with me and argued over some matter (I do not remember what) with that bleak pertinacity which I dreaded, for it frightened me, and the memory of all the other near-'scenes' we had had; of his silence when he was angry with me (once he had not spoken to me at all for more than forty-eight hours); of the misery I had seen in his face, and felt on my own; of our rigid estrangement (for we still spoke to each other as if we were strangers who had met and disliked each other at sight): all this depressed me so much that I wept; and because I was very weak I could not stop weeping; and the nurse came in (she was young and pretty: exactly like a Botticelli virgin) and the moment she saw that I was in tears she turned on Richard like a tiger and drove him from the room. I was ashamed that she had seen this trouble, but intensely grateful that she protected me. And as she turned from the door, and Richard's vanishing back, she was still glaring furiously, looking so young and determined, and she said 'HE shan't come back again until he's better-tempered. I'll get you a sleeping-draught, too – ' And then she went away and I lay back on the pillows and wept more than ever.

I was rather ashamed of having this operation. X had a friend who had also become my friend. She belonged to a society I had never met before – the near-stage people; the people who knew People. She was extremely attractive;

slender, supple, boyish; completely amoral and very amorous. Through her I had discovered many modern writers; notably Aldous Huxley, T. F. Powys, D. H. Lawrence, T. S. Eliot, and so on. I now devoured their works, and the literary reviews. She had a very free tongue and enjoyed startling me. Her letters while I was ill were bawdy and entertaining, but she laughed at me for the nature of the operation, and I was shy about it.

After I had been in the home for about a week Richard thought I ought to come out, but the woman surgeon said I was too weak and that I must stay at least another four or five days, and then I must not at once return to housework and domesticity. X's friend, R., wrote to me suggesting that when I came out I should go with her to Dorset, to a small village she had heard of where T. F. Powys lived. We would stay in a cottage there. I was immediately determined to go.

Richard protested but the doctor insisted that I should go away. Richard wanted me to go to Norfolk; but R. said that the cottage was just the right place: a woman would cook for us; it had a bathroom and indoor sanitation; it was convenient, cheap, quiet, and Richard could come down at the weekend. My mother thought it sounded exactly what I needed, and so Richard was overborne, and we went.

On the day before we were to leave I got up for the first time. I could scarcely stand, but I went in a hired car through the Park to the Army and Navy Stores, where I bought a pair of men's flannel trousers. R. had said that we could wear these clothes down in Dorset, and the idea amused me. Returning to the home I put them on, and watched by amused nurses I tottered downstairs again, and into the car in my trousers, and off to drive round the

Park again. It was November, but the air was mild and the sun shone. I felt dizzy but contented.

The next day I was driven to Waterloo station where I met R. and we got into a third-class carriage for Wool, in Dorset. We took two suitcases, and I took a wooden box full of books, and a portable gramophone with a few records; some dance tunes, and the 'Siegfried Idyll', and a few recordings of lieder sung by Gerhardt.

It was evening by the time we arrived at the village, and when we found the cottage it turned out to be a thatch and stone-built one, with a small living-room and the stairs leading into the big bedroom and a smaller room beyond. There was an earth closet at the end of the garden, next to the pigsty. All water was drawn from a well. In the grate a fine fire burned and although I could scarcely stand, I was so tired and felt so strangely light-headed, we sat down to a meal of strong tea and biscuits, and later on we had some Bovril and cheese, and then went upstairs to bed.

The extraordinary pleasure of sleeping alone: I have never been happier, never known a greater rapture in my life that I knew when I shut the door of my bedroom that night! I lay in bed and by the light of the candle looked around the tiny room: sloping ceiling, minute window, the overhanging eyebrow of thatch above it; a text on the wall above the washstand said 'GOD IS LOVE'. I blew out the candle and lay on my back, listening to the owls until I fell asleep.

[VI]

When I read what I have written so far, and remember what more there is to write, it puzzles me to know why I can endure myself. Everything told here is so *mean*; even the suffering, even the bewilderment is mediocre; except for the pitiful loss I suffered when my first love was taken from me – that, I know, was not in any way little; it had anguish in it, and true tragedy. But except for that, as I have shown them, and as I sometimes see them, the events of my life have been paltry events, and base too, and of little worth.

Yet there is something else, although I do not know how to convey it; something which makes the 'crisis' I described at the beginning of this document possible to believe. I have tried to discover it at its beginning, in my early childhood, for there – one would think – it should show most clearly. But I do not find it.

'Was I a good child?' I asked my mother lately, and she said, 'Yes, you were very, very good.' And I tried to remember how that showed itself.

All I could remember were little, paltry things, tainted with self-consciousness, with something very much like hypocrisy. For instance, the old woman who opened the door at school: she was called Mrs Burrows and she told me once that her husband was a cripple, and could only go out in a bath-chair. I believe I did feel a genuine impulse of pity and concern, but it was swallowed up almost instantly in my passionate desire to show myself charitable.

116

I bought (heaven help me! I suppose the money was saved from Xmas presents, or the Easter guinea my grandmother gave me) the miniature bottles of Bovril one could get in those days. I have a feeling that they cost a farthing each, but that is surely not possible? At any rate, they were very cheap indeed, and so small that I do not suppose one could make more than one cup of soup from one bottle.

These I would present to Mrs Burrows, with much formality, and beg her to give her husband a hot drink of soup to nourish him ...

I do not remember that she laughed at me, or that she became annoyed; but I don't think she was as much impressed by my goodness as I expected, for I don't remember any very great pleasure from giving them to her, although I do remember feeling a passionate desire to buy one of the little bottles and take it to school – hoping, I suppose, that this time she would really look at me with awe and emotion.

I did curious things sometimes; I forced myself to have physical contact with poor children, friends of the servants, or children who played in the mews at the back of our house, or the little boy who was brought in to shelter when there was an air raid. I loathed their smell, and the feeling of their skin or hair; but I knew stories of the saints, and I believed that I was equally a saint when I touched one of these children. I did *believe* this. I must have been a small, walking hell of spiritual pride when I was a child. And not only when I was a child, either.

My mother has always been extravagantly generous; some of that comes from a natural overflowing, healthy generosity and some from the same source as mine – cowardice. Some few times in my life, I hope, I have been naturally generous; but many, many times that I remember

117

with horror and shame I have bribed, and played the hypocrite, and almost known it, and then deliberately deceived myself into the bargain.

What, then, was ever good in me?

I do not know. Unless it was the will to be good. Pascal made Christ say 'Thou wouldst not seek Me if thou hadst not already found Me.' My desire to be good was not only a desire to be thought good. It was not even tainted with that – although I was almost filled to capacity with that dreadful ambition. In some one place in me there has always been an uncontaminated desire to be good. That is purely a matter of grace, as the theologians call it; it is the only explanation I have of how I come to be still able to live with myself.

When I woke in the morning, in that cottage in Dorset, I lay in my unshared bed exulting. I heard R. begin to get up. We talked through the closed door. She went downstairs and soon after I followed. I was shaky still, but I was only concerned that she should not suspect it, for she suggested that we should go for a walk 'Just a little way over the hill' to see two sisters of T. F. Powys, who lived somewhere near the sea, she thought; and then would would go on to see a brother of his, who lived not far away, also near the sea; and then we would make our way down to the village and call on T. F. Powys himself.

R. had been brought to see him by a young man she had been in love with. She only had a vague remembrance of the geography of the place but she was sure nothing was very far away. We would take a few biscuits and start off. And so we did.

We walked until above five that evening; I felt extremely ill after a time. I could scarcely drag myself along by the time we were coming down the hill towards T. F. Powys's house. I think, allowing for mistakes we made in finding the places we were to visit, that we must have covered about ten miles; or at least eight. I scarcely realized where I was, and scarcely saw T. F. Powys and his wife; we sat by a fire and drank some tea, I remember, and R. talked gaily and with a great deal of sparkle. I scarcely spoke a word, and at last we got up and walked the last little distance to our cottage. There I still would not admit that I was tired, and we sat by the fire until a decent hour for going to bed; I buoyed myself by remembering that I would again sleep alone. But, perhaps because I was so deadly tired, when I got to my room I suddenly remembered that this was only a brief holiday. I would have to go back to Richard.

I slept badly that night, and next morning I admitted that I did not think I could walk so far that day. R. was charming; she was delighted to stay in the village. She played tunes on the gramophone and danced to it – doing fine high-kicks that touched the beam of the ceiling. She said we must buy pipes and smoke tobacco: George Sand, she thought, had smoked a pipe; and *she* had worn trousers. We would walk, next day, to the neighbouring village and buy pipes and some twist.

So two days passed, and half the third. In the afternoon I began again to worry about returning to London and to Richard.

On the morning of the fourth day I wrote a letter telling him that I would never go back to him. This I carried in my trouser pocket when R. and I walked up over the hill to visit the two ladies again. I sat in the sitting-room, while the artist-sister talked to R. about sitting for her portrait; and I felt the letter in my pocket, and wondered. We came back over the hill at last, and I went to the village post office and dropped my letter in the box.

That evening, as we tried to smoke our pipes, I told R. what I had done. She was not at all shocked; she laughed and said she supposed Richard would arrive down, and what would I do then?

I replied that I should steadfastly refuse to go back to him.

She nodded: 'He is very dull,' she said, 'He's quite the wrong person for you, darling; I don't know *what* sort of a man you would like? Perhaps you'd rather have a woman?'

This startled me considerably, but it delighted me too. X had forbidden me to tell anyone at all about our relationship; and except for the priest of St Patrick's, Soho, I had kept faithfully the promise I gave her. R. was her friend. Obviously I could not even hint it to her. But I was young enough and indiscreet enough to ask what she felt about X. And R. was sophisticated, and although she had long realized our relationship, she said nothing about it, but laughed, and admitted that she had longed for X to fall in love with her, for ages and ages she had hoped for it, but X never would, she knew – and so she gave herself no concern about it.

'Do you love women, then?' I asked innocently.

R. looked at me oddly, and then nodded; 'Anything that comes!' she said gaily.

We sat by the fire and read poetry aloud to each other; we discussed the Immortality of the Soul and R. was emphatically of the opinion that it was impossible; I was unsure, but for the sake of argument maintained the theory. We discussed whether Man was capable of Moral Goodness; and R. proved succinctly that he was not. We discussed Blake's theology, and the dogma of the Virgin Birth. I half-heartedly defended the Catholic position, but

I was a little ashamed of it when R. laughed at it so cheerfully.

The next day a note arrived from Richard to say that he would be coming down on Saturday, the day after his letter came.

We went off to the neighbouring village to book a room for him at the inn.

He came, wearing town trousers because he had come straight from the office. He looked completely out of place. He was very pale and serious, and he was embarrassed to find R. there; he had only met her once or twice and he had never liked her. He loathed her husband (who was indeed loathsome) and he had practically forbidden me to know them any longer. Now he was confronted by her, and he was considerably abashed.

I scribbled on a copy of the *New Statesman* 'Do not leave us alone!' and gave it to R. She therefore stayed with us until the evening; and we took Richard for that long walk; visiting the sisters, visiting the brother and his wife, visiting T. F. Powys. By now I had come to revere T. F. Powys profoundly; I relied implicitly on his judgement; I wanted him to pronounce on Richard. We stayed there for tea and supper. As we walked back in the dark towards the cottage, Richard said to R., 'Will you please let me talk to my wife alone?' And R. said she would. I could do nothing. Richard and I sat opposite each other in the cottage, while R. went for a walk. Our conversation was halting and awkward. Richard made no attempt to make love to me; he spoke angrily, sourly; he asserted that I 'could not do it', and reminded me that we were Catholics and could not break our marriage. In my new delights, in my liberty, I felt nothing but scorn for this, and anger at his coldness. Throughout the day I had seen him with the people I now admired and esteemed above all people I had ever met. They talked about books, about poetry, about ideas; Richard waved his hand at me in one of the gestures I disliked – I hated all his gestures, of an Englishman educated abroad, who had learned these gesticulations by rote – using them without any natural need to – they were stilted, mannerless gestures, and I abhorred them. I gazed at him with dislike and repulsion, and he stared back at me without a trace of love in his expression.

At last he got up to go. I followed him to the door and then he turned and looked at me with a strange kind of cold lust that I have never seen on any face since, thank God; and he stood silently, looking at me so, until I said 'Good night,' and he replied, 'I will write to you. Good night.' And he went away.

R. came back much later, but all the time between I spent in sitting by the fire, feeling strangely shaky and yet light-hearted. When she came back I said I was very happy, and she remarked, rather reprovingly, that Richard had looked very ill, and she had felt sorry for him; I had treated him badly, she said, not to let him speak to me alone until right at the end. I felt guilty and went up to bed. Once in my room I thought, 'If I had not refused to speak alone to him until I had seen him beside all these others, I might have been frightened into going back, or I might have been in some way overpowered by him,' and I remembered that strange, cold stare of his, and felt so sick that I scarcely dared get into bed. In the morning my first thought was 'By now he has got into the train and gone away!' And I felt a little compunction, a little shadowy feeling of *being married* to him; but it went away before it did me any mischief.

Watching some farm labourers, with guns and dogs,

122

deploy themselves over the field on this Sunday afternoon, hoping to shoot rabbits, I wonder whether they remember, on Monday, Tuesday, Wednesday, and on through the dull week, the particular aspect of freedom and pleasure the field wears for them today?

For many years after the day that Richard left, I stayed in this Dorset village; but I do not know that it ever wore such a glory again. It was an extraordinary place: extraordinary things happened there and extraordinary people were to be found there; and to everyone according to his capacity it gave according to his need. But I do not know that, for me, it ever wore such a bright glory as it wore the day after Richard had gone back to London.

Of course, my decision to leave Richard caused a great stir in my family; no doubt it did in his too, but I did not know about that until later, when it was scarcely at all real to me. My sister immediately asked him down to stay with her in the country.

Her attitude to my marriage had been inconsistent; after the first conversation, which had precipitated me into the civil marriage, she had changed her attitude completely. Although she turned up at the Registry Office she wore anything but a benign aspect, and when she was asked to sign as a witness she announced 'My husband has forbidden me to countenance this marriage' – which disconcerted the Registrar considerably. Richard was delighted because all the eccentricities of my family entertained him and the whole scene, he told me, was singularly like something in a Russian play – and he admired Russian plays. My mother was not so well-pleased, although I do not think she was in any way alarmed by the incident, nor yet embarrassed by it, but she thought it would hurt my feelings. I do not remember that

123

it did; I was so tired and over-excited by the drive of the night before that I scarcely noticed it, and when Richard told me it had delighted him I was glad of that, and thought of it no more. Now, however, she wrote me a very angry letter, and asked Richard to stay with her.

After that weekend he wrote to me, telling me some of the advice she had given him and some of the things she had told him about me; also in his letter there were other things which he did not know that he was quoting, but which I recognized very well. It was evident that the new situation had stimulated her a great deal.

My mother wrote very kindly, but reproachfully, and in great anxiety. I felt for a moment unhappy because of her letter, but it went away and was replaced by my constant feeling, at that time, of infinite lightness and liberty of spirit. I was tranquil and I felt physically very strong and well. I thought nothing could hurt me now. I had escaped for ever. And this was almost true; for although I could not escape from the consequences of the confusion in which I had lived, and there was a long time to be spent before I managed to moult away my draggled adolescence, yet from that time onwards I had a free spirit inside me.

I refused to go back to London yet awhile; I argued that if, as they said, my balance had been upset by the experience of being married (an odd statement, I thought then, but perhaps they were right) then it would be sensible to stay away for a while, and my mother agreed, and continued to send me my allowance, which at my marriage had been increased to £300 a year.

It was very little money for me to live on, who had never lived on my own money in my life. But I did not know that, and R. and I lived mainly on biscuits and Bovril, with sometimes some sausages and a lard-cake as a treat.

We spent no money except on our food and lodging. In those days a glass of beer was a riotous feast. We drank mostly tea, and well-water, although one evening, when X came down for the weekend and we decided to have a Saturday night feast, we bought a quarter bottle of gin, one of brandy and one of rum at the local inn, and those we poured into a bowl and stirred with a red-hot poker; then we drank each our share. I was sick almost at once; R. got very merry and sang and X got extremely drunk and argued about religion – I could not argue, fortunately, for I felt very ill; but I remember that R. declared that the Virgin Mary was nothing but a whore, and X slapped her face and ran out of the cottage into the darkness. I sat mutely by the fire and R. became sober instantly, and was overwhelmed with remorse. Then I went to bed and much later heard the other two making it up with mutual, rather stiff apologies. And then X came to bed in my room, where we shared my double-bed and I quite forgot about the happiness of lying alone.

R. went back to London for a while and I lived on by myself; seeing the Powyses every day, now one, now all of them and borrowing books as fast as I could from them all. I read *Gil Blas*, Voltaire, Richardson, Smollett, Rousseau, various new American authors, David Garnett, Sylvia Townsend Warner, *King Lear*, and an immensity of poetry, besides Lucian and William Blake, both of whom I had brought down with me. I had what we knew as 'Powys Mania' very severely; everything all of them said was beautiful and wise and true. I asked T. F. P. what he thought of Richard, and when he said 'Well, my dear, I thought he was a very nice young man but not the sort of young man who would get on very well with our country manners,' that dissolved, instantly and as I thought for ever, all ties between Richard and me. God had spoken. I cheerfully obeyed.

But Christmas came, and I was still partly a Catholic. I went to confession and to Midnight Mass, taking one of the Powys sisters with me on that lovely drive through the darkness to Bindon Abbey. My Mass was an act of poetry; I experienced it through her eyes and ears and felt it only in her heart. A romantic, poetic appreciation of the situation – I was very happy and quite untroubled. I do not in the least remember my confession. I cannot possibly have confessed truthfully, for I had absolution and never disturbed myself in the least about the rights and wrongs of it.

After Christmas the New Year, and R. sent me a message to go straight to London to the Three Arts Ball to which she was taking a party. I went at once. My mother was away and my sister and her husband were staying in her flat. I went there at about six in the morning and when I saw them at breakfast they were very cross. I did not in the least care. After two or three days I went back to Dorset.

So, now it was 1926, and in May I would be twenty. Nothing had been settled; Richard still said stubbornly that he would wait; I was a little unhinged; soon I would return to my senses and go back to him; till then, he would wait. My sister told me that this would infallibly work; my mother shook her head, but there was nothing she could do. As the weeks went by and I stayed in Dorset my mother's letters became more urgent and my sister's more angry; and at last I was forced to go to London to have an interview with Richard. I went up and stayed proudly at the Goring Hotel, which was near my mother's flat. It was a very expensive and grand hotel and I was extremely frightened to be there by myself, but the gesture worked; it made me feel independent and glorious and Richard was considerably diminished by having to see me there.

We had one or two consultations together, and at the last one I convinced him that I would not go back to him. I could see that in his face; he no longer looked at me coldly, but instead he looked at me with longing and almost with love. He felt that he had lost me and I think at that time he minded it.

My mother was very kind to me but very bewildered; she could not believe that I had done this by myself: she thought that T. F. Powys (whom I looked upon as being as venerable as Socrates – a blend of Socrates, William Blake and God the Father) had seduced me. I had great difficulty to persuade her that this was not so.

I returned to Dorset.

I stayed in the cottage by myself for a while; then X came down and we had a very happy weekend in love together. Sometime later R. came to stay with me, and while we were sitting at lunch one day there was a knock at the door and a middle-aged man opened it and looked in and asked 'Is this where Tommy Tomlin stays?' R. sprang up and began to explain that it was indeed the cottage he had found and in which he had stayed; but now he was away and we had hired it. The middle-aged man came into the room, followed by a peculiarly handsome young man. R. told them both to sit down, and we shared our lunch with them while the middle-aged man talked.

He was, he said, a friend of Tommy Tomlin's: his name was Oliver Lodge. This young man was called Sydney Sheppard. The young man blushed. He had not ceased to stare at R. ever since he had arrived. He was curiously good-looking, I thought; a Babylonian countenance; his hair profoundly black and curly; his eyes brilliant, slanting, peat-coloured, or were they grey-hazel? His complexion was brilliantly ivory-coloured, with two neatly-drawn patches of raspberry-red. His hands were large and brown. He wore rough tweed plus-fours, as most artistic young men did just then, and a very old brownish felt hat with the brim flattened; a dirty hat, and he kept it on. In his hands he clasped an extremely thick stick.

Oliver Lodge was expansive and talked with immense eloquence; every sentence was amorous and heavily ornamented with quotations from the Elizabethan poets. I felt embarrassed by him and desperately inclined to giggle; so, I could see, did R. After one exchange of glances we did not dare to look at one another. Oliver talked mostly to me and Sydney kept silence and stared at R. who set herself out to tease and excite him. She chattered, she gazed, she bitched; I watched from the corner of my eye, and felt very jealous of Sydney Sheppard. Oliver at last said they must go, but Sydney growled out, speaking with extraordinary and deliberate slowness, that they would see us again. Then they went.

R. threw herself back in the wicker armchair and began to laugh.

'A conquest! A conquest, darling! Now you will be the daughter-in-law of old Oliver Lodge!'

I was highly indignant and I felt foolish into the bargain. We quarrelled briskly for a while and then it all melted away into playing the gramophone and practising high-kicks.

Next day an envelope arrived, addressed in an affected, fine handwriting *To The Ladies Staying at Mrs Wallis's Cottage, Chaldon Herring, Dorchester*, and inside a letter, in the same hand, asking if they might visit us again on their way back to London.

They came in the morning and in a few moments Sydney and R. went off for a walk. I looked at Oliver in despair. How should I manage to keep up a conversation? He suggested a walk in another direction, adding jocosely that I would not grudge Sydney his fortune, would I? I hastily said No. Oliver went on to tell me that the boy was only twenty, and that he had confided that he had fallen desperately in love with R. and must at all costs see her again immediately. 'He is a virgin – ' Oliver added proudly. 'She has a wonderful opportunity – ' and then he said 'Bless her!' in the voice of a patriarch.

We started out across the field-path, but Oliver soon began to suspect that the cows were not alone in the field; 'There is a bull among them; I am sure of it – Your beauty torn and destroyed by the cruel violence of a bull. Or do you know from experience that it is Zeus himself?'

I replied that they were all cows, and there was a stile further on.

'A stile!' he exclaimed in ecstasy. And we went on till we reached it.

As I got over, athletically enough in my trousers, Oliver groaned very loudly and clasped his hands in despair: 'Alas! Alas! Eheu! Now that ladies wear these heathen garments, we are cheated of all sight of bliss!' he said. I did not in the least understand what he meant until he reached out a hand and placed it firmly on my stomach and went on, 'Do you wear these things to protect yourself from the ravishers in this village? It is clear that T. F. Powys has frightened all you young ladies – Perhaps you are right – but would you not, for me, *for me*, put on the delicate draperies that at least promise bliss?'

I was deeply embarrassed and turned away abruptly, but he giggled delightedly and trotted after me along the high-road: 'Come, live with me and be my Love, And we will all the pleasures prove – '

What should I do with him? I took him up to T. F. Powys's house and established him there and returned to my cottage.

R. and Sydney were there before me, sitting one on either side of the fireplace, apparently in silence. Sydney looked morosely at me and R. laughed and asked what I had done with Oliver.

'Left him at Beth-Car,' I said.

Sydney raised his head and looked at me severely, 'You should be kind to him,' he said heavily. 'He hoped great things from your indulgence.'

R. laughed but I looked at her helplessly. 'Will you come with me to fetch him?' I asked, and later she told me that she had never in her life heard such imploring anguish in any human voice.

They both came with me and we spent some time at the house, drinking gin and milk, which T. F. P. favoured at that time. And after a hasty lunch the two left to walk to Wool station. We went with them as far as the next village, and Sydney carefully wrote down R.'s name and address in London, while Oliver in a fine speech declared that he had already learnt all he could of my name and circumstances from the Powyses. Then, after Oliver had kissed our hands and quoted extensively from Blake (I think) they went off, and we turned for home.

'Could you love Sydney?' I asked R.

'Yes,' she said promptly, 'I shall.' So I said no more.

When she left for London, two days later, I realized dimly that I felt rather oddly towards her; but I was still absorbed by loving X and I gave no serious thought to anything else.

But R. and I had discovered that there was a peculiar local brand of spirits to be bought at the neighbouring village, in quarter-bottles, and we had bought gin and whisky there fairly often, although one small bottle lasted us as much as two days. When she had gone I continued the custom of walking to that pub and drinking a tankard of brown ale and buying a small bottle of gin or whisky. Every night, now, I drank a little measure of spirits and smoked, with considerable difficulty, a pipe of twist tobacco.

I visited London fairly often, and at last got a flat in Bloomsbury, where I stayed sometimes for a month or six weeks on end; but I was always very homesick for Chaldon. Time stretches out like elastic at that age: I think perhaps I only had that flat, the first time, for about two months. Then, after a series of family rows, I was compelled to travel abroad with my mother. The journey was to bring me to my senses; wean me from Chaldon; make me long to return to Richard. It did none of those things, but it did make me drink more steadily, and put reliance on drink.

For I was unhappy and bored, alone with my mother. I was still half a Catholic. We went to Rome and there met a Catholic family who roused me to a positive antagonism to the Church. I concentrated all my attention on classical Rome and would not so much as look at any Catholic holy places except with disdain and dislike.

We visited Rome, then, and Portofino and Cap d'Antibes and ended up in Paris. Then we returned to England, and I declared, as was the truth, that I was more than ever determined not to return to Richard.

I had a brief love affair with a man, in London, which resulted in my becoming pregnant. I was wholly delighted

131

with this. I had been happy; I wanted a daughter; it never occurred to me seriously that it might be a son. Just after Christmas, in 1926, I was sure that I was pregnant, and came to London (I had spent Christmas at Chaldon) to verify it. The doctors agreed. Then I sent for Richard and told him. This was in one of the hotel rooms at St James's Court. I remember that he walked across to the window and stood, staring down the seven storeys to the street below; and then he turned, his face deadly pale, and said: 'All right. If you will come back to me I'll accept it as my child.'

That this was generous of him, and perhaps nobly generous, never occurred to me. I was completely self-centred and I did not so much as think of him. I was angry and affronted, and told him at once that I should never *dream* of having my child brought up in his house, or thinking that he was her father. I gazed at him, seeing that he grew even paler, and not a shadow of compassion came into my heart. He went to the door then, and said all right, he would go; if I needed him, I must tell him – I might change my mind –

Never, never, never! I said. And so he went.

I told my mother that I was pregnant. After the first moment of surprise she asked me nothing. It was tacitly agreed, I think, that we should pretend it was Richard's child.

Three months and a half went by, and then, at Chaldon, I slipped down a shallow bank and in about half-an-hour I had a miscarriage. I could not believe it. My whole heart and attention were set on that child; I thought of and desired nothing else in the world. X, whom I had told, was very angry with me and very hurt with me, but had said she would help me to rear it and if I died she would adopt

132

it. I gave no heed to anyone, even to her – my whole thought and my whole love were concentrated on that unborn child. And now it was gone?

I asked T. F. P.'s wife what she thought, and she said she surely thought I had miscarried. She walked with me the two miles or so to the local doctor, a noisy, ignorant old man, who asked a few questions and gave me some medicine and said he supposed that it had been a miscarriage.

I had a haemorrhage for three or four days, with considerable pain, and when I was able to I went to London and saw a gynaecologist, who confirmed that I had indeed miscarried.

For about two months I do not remember what happened. And anyhow, I have over-run my story, because during the time that I was in fact pregnant, I had at last managed to persuade Richard to give me a divorce. Because he was still a professing Catholic, I insisted that it must be a nullity, so that the Church could stretch a point and acknowledge it. This was accomplished, while I still had the child in my belly, by the testimony of the woman doctor who had operated on me and removed my hymen: that disposed of the difficulty of my not being *virgo intacta*. The doctor who examined me for the Law gave me only a very cursory examination, and did not look at my belly or my breasts. So I stood up in Court and swore and thought no harm; and I do not now think harm of that, although Richard later left the Church himself, and we might have saved all that trouble and embarrassment.

The Catholic Church, too, insisted on a full legal hearing at their own court; my lawyer attended with me, and I had to perjure myself all over again, with all the attendant business of bell, book and candle. And at last the

133

dispensation was obtained and Richard was free; and the decree nisi was given, and on that same evening – in line with the manners of those days – Richard and I went to see a musical comedy which we both very much disliked, and went on afterwards to dance at the Café de Paris. He came back with me, I remember, to my flat in Bloomsbury, and wanted to lie with me there, but although I felt it would be the fitting thing to do, I was too miserable, by then, for the loss of my baby to bother with doing things in style. So he went away; taking with him a drawing of me naked, which Eric Gill had made some time earlier.

I have missed out a good deal, I see; thanks to Oliver Lodge, to whom I have become accustomed and who considered himself in love with me (among many other people he also loved) I had begun to sit for the figure to him and to Gill and occasionally to others. Gill exhibited some of the drawings he made of me, and two of them were given to me. Richard stole one of them that night, but I got it back later on.

There are many things that must be missed out. It was an indescribably crowded time. I was still in love with X but steadily unfaithful to her. I lay with many people while I had the Bloomsbury flat: men and girls; I do not think I gave much pleasure to anyone, although sometimes maybe I did. X gave me a little typewriter and I used to spend long May evenings in London trying to write poems and stories. They were always very bad, but I was confident that I was a poet. I do not in the least know why I thought so.

X used to visit me very often, and we always made love and were always extremely happy. She brought sometimes a half-bottle of whisky and always some wine; or we dined out and invariably shared a half-bottle, and followed it with brandy. But I did not then drink much by myself.

I still went down to Chaldon, and in 1927 I spent a summer there in another cottage, while Betty Muntz had Mrs Wallis's for herself. She made many drawings of me when we were on the shore, bathing. I grew brown and apparently strong, but at the end of that summer I had a sharp attack of pneumonia. During that summer I scarcely drank at all, except when Sydney, by then in love with me, or Oliver, or some of the others came to see me. I found that if I could become a little drunk, when they wanted to make love to me, I was better able to deal masterfully with the situation; I did not drink to make myself in desire; I never needed to do that; and I did not drink to dull myself – but I drank because it made me feel secure and self-confident and less shy. I was always pestered by an over-mastering shyness, so that if anyone spoke to me intimately or tried to make me talk so, I became half-idiotic: *unless* I could be a little drunk. And many famous people came down to Chaldon then; people whose work I revered and whose company I longed to feel at home in. But I could not lose my self-consciousness unless and until I was a little drunk. So I drank –

But even then it was not at all difficult to do without it, although I felt inferior and incompetent whenever I did. But fatigue or boredom or something else to do could easily prevent me from bothering to go to the pub for a bottle. Until that Christmas when my brother-in-law sent me down a small case containing two bottles each of whisky and gin and a bottle of sherry and a bottle of port. This was totally unexpected and amazing. I meant to give most of it away, and did indeed give the port and a bottle of gin, but then – by myself in the cottage and later with

135

Sydney who walked through the snow from his parents' house in Dorchester – I drank all the whisky and one bottle of gin and the sherry. That was, I think, the beginning of my drinking *alone*, and regularly. I missed it very much when the stuff was finished, and began to buy it for myself.

In 1928 I got into a set, in London, which was dominated by Dorothy Warren; it touched the Augustus John-Nina Hamnett set and a theatrical set too, as well as the border lines of some others. It was far above my financial capacity, but I enjoyed it for a little, only I was hampered by my extreme shyness and readiness to be embarrassed. I could only maintain any sort of standing there by being a little drunk all the time.

In that summer I went down to Norfolk and had an affair with a girl – a strange, romantic creature who rode racehorses, had lived in fairs, and who enchanted me because of the profound contrast between her and everyone else I had been with recently. I took her down to Chaldon once, and I remember that we were very happy there. But X, with whom I was still in love, was made more miserable by this aberration than by any of the others; and when at last I broke free from it and returned to her, our relationship had been badly damaged and we were both often unhappy.

The following summer X and I went to Italy; at Portofino I remember noticing with some fear that I was dependent on drink. X told me that we could not afford the hotel we were staying at unless we cut down on all extra expenses: no more cocktails and no more liqueurs, for instance; and no more mid-day drinks. I agreed quite happily, but found that all my attention, all day and especially in the evening at about six, was given to contriving how to wheedle a drink – and on the return journey in the Rome Express I drained the brandy flask, although we drank wine with all our meals.

Returning to England I went down to Chaldon and there met T. F. P.'s elder son, newly returned from East Africa. He was shy and amorous and wanted to make love to me; but his brother also wanted to, which I did not know. The elder one told me of this, and gave me to understand that that was why he did not ask me himself. One evening we sat in my cottage and drank a great deal of gin and he became owlish and I became a little unsure of myself. After a long long confused talk about making love, he suddenly got up and went away. Then he came back and stood on the porch. I was going upstairs to my bed, and I heard him come, and I was glad for I was in love with him, I think. But as I turned to go down the stairs I felt suddenly very dizzy from drink, and dared not go down for fear of being sick. And after a moment or so, he went away.

Talking, shyly and with difficulty, about that later on, he made it clear that he believed I had refused to let him in. I was ashamed, and never explained. Then he returned to Africa, and wrote me a few letters which made everything, on his side, very clear: and then an angry letter. And then I never heard any more, and he was killed.

By that time I was fully aware that I had become a dipsomaniac. Very many small things happened, in strange ways, to show me this. One day, in London, I noticed an advertisement in *The Times*, from a girl who had been at my school and who was in need of money. On an impulse (a foolish one, for I was by then chronically overdrawn and very poor indeed) I wrote to her and she came to see me. She was ugly, tall, intense and I was afraid of her. She had supper at my flat and later I offered her

137

liqueur brandy, which I was drinking regularly by then. She had not had wine and she now refused brandy. I drank it. Time went on while we talked and I drank; and then she asked if she might stay the night; and I reluctantly said she might, and made myself a bed on a chair. She sat up for a very long time, and finally said, far too earnestly: 'May I say something? I know what I am talking about. I don't suppose I shall ever see you again, so it won't matter if you are offended. You are drinking far too much. My father died of drink and I have a horror of it. I do beg and implore you not to drink any more – ever again – '

As I remember it, it was a very sharp shock to me, but everything – shock, indignation, fear – was swamped by my instant reaction of embarrassment. I don't know what I said. I think I laughed and pretended it was all a rather bad taste joke. She fell silent and went off to bed, and left next morning, and I have never seen her again.

But this incident made me decide to go to the doctor and tell him; with the result that I have already recounted.

There are some – not so much excuses as explanations of how I had come to be so sick. It was not wholly shyness, although I think probably that alone might have driven me as far as I had gone. But I had suffered a great deal from period pains, ever since adolescence; and I had suffered for a long time from violent, excrutiating neuralgia, for which I had discovered strong red burgundy to be a specific. This had actually been recommended to me by doctors, and supplied to me by my mother in her kindness. I had also at one time suffered from anaemia and been ordered to have red wine and 'fresh, warm calves' liver' – which last had so nauseated me that I had bribed myself to take it by allowing myself to wash it down with a bumper of Pommard directly afterwards. I had, also, gone about in a society which at that time prided itself on Knowing A Lot About Wine; and I had genuinely liked and appreciated good wine myself. None of these things *excuse*, but I think perhaps they *explain* the state I had reached, and how I had come so far.

I do not think that what are called 'sexual aberrations' had anything at all to do with my state at that time. I was naturally more inclined to love women than men; I found deep pleasure, true pleasure and complete satisfaction from making love with women, and less complete pleasure, but still good pleasure, from being made love to by men. I did not ever really and completely make love with men: but with women I was released and happy, and I gave happiness and pleasure; and I did not need any kind of help from drink, to make me feel competent and secure in making love.

After my visit to the doctor, and a talk, also recounted earlier, with the 'famous man', and my second visit to the doctor, I was very near to despair. X, by then, had talked to me seriously about the danger of becoming addicted to drink. Her mother was, and she feared it for herself, and she had, at that time, a half-formed fear that she had drawn me into it – as, indeed, she had – so far as any one person is able to be responsible for another person's offence: and that, I am afraid, is very far. For I must have done a great deal of harm myself, to other people. I know that I have; to two at least, and it is only by some strange stroke of mercy that I have not ruined many more that I know of; and I am afraid, often very much afraid, that that sentence in the Bible about the millstone applies inevitably to me.

So, very near to despair, and already marking my diaries 'DD' and so on, and striving very weakly and in great

139

shame against it; I came to the year which began my deepest and most sure happiness, my richness, my secure life of love: and during the next *nineteen years* I was fighting feebly, often desperately, and never with any honourable success, against this fiendish, abhorrent weakness. And all that time my Love beside me, and I silent and without a word to her about it. I think, now, that that was right, although I am not sure that the motive for it was always unadulterated ... Yes, I think I am sure: I think that when I decided to myself, the night she first came to me, when I was later lying alone and thinking of this unbelievable, startling happiness, and of the complications and pain it must bring with it, when I then reviewed my own state, recognizing very clearly its horror and hopelessness, I decided that if I told her now, it would mean that, whether our love lasted long or only for a while, for all the time we had it she would be in fear for me, in horror perhaps; and sharing what I had found to be as nearly as anything unbearable fear and degradation.

I decided then, and stuck to it until about a week ago when I told her all of this, that I should never never tell her, but fight it as best I might – and perhaps, I told myself in bitter shame and grief, perhaps now that someone so wholly, so transparently good, possessed of the utmost integrity, of passion and fidelity and candour and of what, even then, I knew to be extraordinary intellectual power and virtue: perhaps if *she* loves me, I shall pull myself up out of this stinking bog, this horror and shame – perhaps I shall be a poet, I said; as she tells me she believes I may be – perhaps I shall live, at last – and be able to give her a good life.

I thought that, but I do not know that I hoped it. I thought it and meant to try for it; and to some extent I did try. At least, I continued without very many breaks to fight hard for it; and the breaks were never total collapses, I think: that is to say, I do not think I ever gave up the intention of fighting it, although I often gave up hope of winning.

And so I came to this year which was truly a beginning, and which will never have an ending, although END seems to be written large and clear about it just now. But that is a different end from any she yet knows about: and what she does know about is certainly in no way, in no sense of the word an End.

Julian of Norwich says what at this moment of writing is very much in my mind: 'Our failing is dreadful, our falling is shameful, and our dying is sorrowful; but in all this the sweet eye of pity and love is lifted never off us, nor the working of mercy ceaseth.' Please God that may soon be proved to be true in its simplest meaning. But I must wait two more days or so before I can know that.

[VII]

The two days have passed and the third day is almost at an end. I had reason to believe that I had cancer, and now I have seen a specialist and he has told me I have not. It is a curious thing that while I have very much trust, enough, at times, to carry me right over the highest point of obstruction and run me far inshore, on to solid land, so that I easily accept the probability of miracles, and find myself tranquilly established in belief that God is good and that there is, in fact, a 'sweet eye of pity and love' which is never lifted off us: even so, when the comfort has been established and the miracle worked and the tension eased and the storm over – finding myself still securely set on dry ground, I begin to fear and dread the far-off sea, and cannot rest securely because I now do not believe that anything stands between it and me.

So today I have walked about, much of the time at any rate, in a state of terror and almost abject fear: beating off bogeys and horrors, seeing nothing but a weakly mercy which has given me a brief reprieve and gone away – leaving me to wait for the knock on the cell-door . . .

I suppose I was more terrified than I knew. But if I was, then what an infinite grace worked for me, blanketing out that part of my mind or giving me courage. But have I *ever* had courage? I wish I knew if I had.

The year's end of 1929, then, brought me to Chaldon, with the Powys boy returned to East Africa and Sylvia staying in the village. She saw an empty cottage, while she stayed there, and on an impulse of concern for me (I had shown her some poems of mine; very weakly and bad ones, and she had seen good in them or perhaps seen good in me, and become friendly to me) she suggested that she should buy the place and asked whether, if she did, I would live in it and 'keep it warm', so that she might come down from time to time, and stay there a little while, and visit Theodore and Violet. Strangely enough, for in my shyness and awkwardness I do not usually say Yes to any proposal, I instantly said that I would. And she as instantly set about buying it.

It was a small, plain-faced cottage, opposite the village inn; it had two bedrooms and a sitting-room and a long narrow back-kitchen, with a copper in it. And a very good plot of neglected garden ground.

The negotiations over the sale took a long time, but at last it was accomplished and in the Easter of the next year I went down to the village with X and we stayed in lodgings and went there each day for me to dig the garden. In October of that year, 1930, Sylvia moved in, and I went down, on October 4th, with a few oddments of furniture, and found her there, with a duck cooking and one large dubious-looking horse-mushroom which she had picked on the Five Marys that afternoon. We ate that good dinner and drank some Beaujolais and then some brandy that I had brought; and we went to bed. In the morning I came downstairs in my fine silk man's dressing-gown and morocco slippers, and lighted the first fire. It burned very brightly and kindled without trouble.

After about a week, during which I had felt shy and tried to behave as if I were not, while we were talking through the partition between our narrow bedrooms, I said sadly 'I sometimes think I am utterly unloved.' And Sylvia

143

thought she heard heart-break melancholy in my voice, and with that passionate immediacy of succour which matches, through all her character, and makes her have the most purely beautiful heart I have even known – perhaps that has ever existed – she sprang up and came through the connecting door and fell on her knees by my bed and took me in her arms. I do not know what happened then, except that in a moment or so she was in my bed and I was holding her and kissing her and we were already deeply in love – and never since then have we ceased to love each other, and with each year of our joined lives we have loved more, and more truly.

After a little time, that night, I bade her go back to bed, for it was already very late and she had been tired before we went upstairs. And I lay alone in my bed, listening to the inn sign opposite creaking in the stubborn wind that almost always blew across that valley; and I pondered what strange thing, now, had happened; and what I should do; and where I found myself. And I thought of X and knew in my bones that this had dealt a final death to that. And I thought of my own blight, my disease and shame –

Our lives, for the next few weeks, scarcely knew night or day or any change in the hours or weather; we knew nothing except our joy and pleasure and the thousand-and-one, infinitely fine adjustments that we were each making, to fit always closer and closer to each other.

If I had stopped drinking then, I believe I would scarcely have noticed it, for everything was exciting, tense, taxing and well within my powers – the state I was in was exactly like the state I took drink to create for me and in me: but I did not trust myself, by then; I did not think that I could *be myself* without stimulant. I did not dare to try.

144

As a result, then, I drank more and more. I remember that I used to go across to the inn and get quarter- and then half-bottles of whisky, and that I felt great shame sometimes, thinking that the woman who sold me the stuff would know that I drank. But she was a very good, a merciful woman, a rare character to find in the country, and she did not show any sign of understanding my baseness.

Time went on, and all the time I became more happy, and Sylvia did too, I think; and our lives joined up imperceptibly, all along their lengths, so that without thinking about it or arranging it, we remained together and could scarcely endure a day's parting, or an hour's. That is why, now as I write, I feel as though I were looking down into the pit of death; for at this distance of time (I write in June 1949) it is just the same: I cannot bear to be away from her. 'And still from her company I could not go – '

One day an old lover of Sylvia's came to our cottage: he had been a brilliant young man; everyone I had recently met had been in love with him – young men and young women – all except I myself had seen him as beautiful and rare and entrancing. Sylvia had been in love with him, deeply, I think; appreciatively and protectively, and romantically as well. I looked on him with disfavour, for this reason and others, when he came in first, but very soon that ran out of me and I was left with pity and consternation only: for he was going along my path, I could see. He was already more than half destroyed by drink. I listened to him and watched him and my heart turned to stone. After he had gone I went up to my unused bedroom and sat down with my head in my hands; I tried to stir myself to a violent, an overwhelming effort. But the

145

thing is not to be met so – at least, I could not manage it that way: anger, fear, even determination – even the desperate desire to save love itself – do not endure for long enough. If I managed to go through two or three days without drinking, that was all I did, and I do not know whether I even did that.

One evening, somewhere about this time, I was feeling utterly depleted and drained; I could not write; I could not think; I felt inferior, abased, dishevelled in my spirit; and I went upstairs to my room and drank and drank of neat whisky. And then I became very tired and lay down, and felt dizzy, and then sick, and then fell into a stupor.

Sylvia heard sounds from my room and I awoke to find her clasping me in her arms and calling me, half-frantic with fear. I realized what had happened, though I did not know exactly what it was, and hastily got up and said I must have fainted – or perhaps had a migraine. I looked in the glass and saw my face deadly pale and noticed that the pupil of my left eye was considerably larger than the other one. I felt very cold, and collapsed, and went to bed with hot water bottles.

Next day I saw a doctor, and he said maybe it had been a migraine and told me to stay in bed. I nerved myself to it, and next time he came I told him I was drinking too much. 'How much a day?' he asked. I said about a quarter of a bottle, and sometimes a little more; and wine. He told me, then, that he had once been in the same state, and said that no one could cure it but oneself. How? I asked desperately, and he said only by will-power and the intention not to drink. Could he not help me by giving me some sort of drug, I asked, but he said No. Nothing would do but will-power and the intention not to drink.

That left me pretty much as he had found me, except

146

that I took a little comfort because he had been kind. But that wore off, when he could do nothing for me, and after a while, during which I regained my health (I must have had a very strong constitution: it is not the least of my offences that I played that away) I returned to the old way, the old misery, and nothing was changed.

I had one other attack of this sort, as bad, and several lesser ones in the next six or seven years; and always the pupil of my left eye became distended, and I suffered the most agonizing pain over that eye. But each time it cleared up without mishap. Even now, almost two years after I was rescued so strangely, I still sometimes get an enlargement of that pupil and a pain over that eye.

All this time I was unsure whether Sylvia knew. I thought sometimes that she *must* know; I sometimes almost broke my heart about whether or no I should tell her – but always decided that, even if she knew, it was better not to put it into words: while it was unspoken, I thought, it allowed us some chance of keeping good manners between us, even while I was being a brute beast; and once spoken, we should never, perhaps, repair the courtesy between us ... As it turns out, she did not know anything about it, and she says that she has never seen me drunk. I do not think there can be anyone in the world with so much true magnanimity of heart, so much trust and profound compassion of belief in goodness, as she has. I know no one, of all those I now know about who lived in true integrity of heart and spirit, who is so wholly good as she is: and I shall never – no one will ever – see such a one again. And she has loved me and I, to my life's end, love her with all my heart.

After a time at Chaldon, two of the village people we most loved and revered, died: and the place suddenly became changed for us. Not that we loved it, and our little house, the less, but – like Mr Mole in *The Wind in the Willows*, we knew that we must leave the underground burrow and move to live in the world, by the wide river. And at that time, by the grace of the fortune that was ours, we found the perfect house in Norfolk, Frankfort Manor, at Sloley, and it was to let at £50 a year.

It was a long, two-storey house, dating back, perhaps, to the sixteenth century; with a Georgian front door and several of the rooms had been refashioned in that period, and some later. It had a fine brick Dutch gable and two vast attics (making, in fact, a third storey, under the steep thatched roof, which was thatched in the Norfolk manner, with reeds). The garden covered, with a meadow, about three acres: with innumerable fruit trees and roses and two asparagus beds. There were fine trees, tall and stately Spanish chestnuts, and elms, and ash trees and every sort of flowering shrub and soft fruits and a great many rare flowers; it had stables, too, and a large garage, and a curved 'sweep' in front of the house.

It was the loveliest small manor house I have ever seen, and our bedroom had a powder closet, and long low windows with roses all about them; and shoe-rose poppies, tall and romantically pink, growing up to look in at the sitting-room window.

There we lived for the better part of three years, gardening and loving and writing. And for the first week or so I did not drink and we were both well and as happy as we have ever been. After that I fell back.

In one sense, I suppose, nothing that happens in a life is a digression; the people who believe they see a clear pattern in their own or someone else's life are in fact seeing only part of the whole, or can only see certain primary colours and from these trace a far simpler design than is in fact there. And in trying to describe a life, even parts of a life, nothing (in this sense) can be a digression: so it is not out of place to break off here and talk about that song 'L'heure exquise'.

Because it has just been sung, over the radio, and Sylvia has called out to me 'Don't come in yet; you can't hear this' – which is true: or true that I do not willingly hear it, because it reminds me –

What that single-hearted song reminds me of is *youth*. I do not often remember it clearly; I do not often, that is to say, experience it again; like the taste of strawberries in early June; in late October it is lost – nothing can make one's palate recall it.

'L'heure exquise' – I had a gramophone record of it, which X gave me in 1924, just after we had fallen in love. I believe it was sung by Claire Dux. I remember, but as if I were now dead, sitting in the arm-chair in the drawing-room at St James's Court, and X sitting opposite to me, and then getting up, during the course of the song, and walking to the window alongside me and looking out. Her rather heavy face, with its noble seventeenth-century nose and the beautiful arch of forehead (or is it brow, just above the eyeball?) looked most grave, most moved as she stared out of the window and the woman on the record sang so poignantly: and then she turned towards me and put her large, very white hand on my shoulder and said 'I love you' – and my whole body was swept with little, bright tremors; and I suddenly thought, very vividly indeed, 'This is my youth!'

That is why I dare not hear that song; because of Keats's poem: 'Too happy, happy tree ... '

But it is not because of that love, or of any particular

149

love, that I cannot bear to hear it. It is because youth, I suppose, is never lost and never, at this distance, appears to have been spent. One's life is so very long (I am forty-three as I write this); one's experience so *much*; it is as if one were a cistern, filled by the rain running off the roof: very clear and cool and pure, always, the water that runs in, and it is not very often that any is drawn off; and it is as if the cistern, which is oneself, were thinking sometimes of the first showers of rainwater that ever flowed in – how miraculously cool and soft and valuable that water seemed; how little there was, safely stored there in one's own dark depths; and then more and more rains, showers or storms or drizzling downpours; and what has happened to that first, that purest of all cool water? Lying right down at the bottom, one might think if one were a cistern; it will never be drawn off – never – never – And yet, the tap (if anyone comes to turn it) is right down at the bottom, and that is the very layer which is first drawn off.

As if water remained stored in layers! But that is how my mind works, taking images and setting them a little awry: not as St Teresa would use them – so careful of her dearest image.

At Frankfort Manor, then, we lived in a kind of solemn, fairy-story splendour. The first spring and summer brought nothing but miraculous days. Every day a fresh discovery: one day I found white currants; another day we discovered first one, then another, then a nest of 'rough' cats, living in the little tumble-down outhouses; another day we started birds'-nesting and found a greenfinch's nest, and many others; another day, in the evening, we met a hedgehog walking up the drive; another day, in full sun, I was picking green peas into a colander and saw the earth near my feet heaving, and a mole emerged, and I caught it instantly, in the colander, and carried it in to Sylvia, who was writing in her room, and set it down beside the typewriter on her table. And so on – every day, every evening, every night and every dawn there was some new, strange beauty or curiosity or discovery. And we were very very happy.

But in my room, with books all round me and working hard at poetry every evening for hours on end, I still fought a constant, and a constantly lost, battle against that accursed habit. After a while I kept a bottle of whisky in my cupboard there, as well as a bottle in the dining-room cupboard; and I drank by day too, in the morning often and sometimes all through the day. Whenever we went out for picnics or excursions in the car I drank at pubs; we both did, but for Sylvia it was an accompaniment to a meal or a pleasure-party, while for me it was a constant, often desperate desire for the stuff, and a counting of the moments till I got it, and then a counting of the moments till I could reasonably have another one. And whenever I had to meet people, or they came to stay, or we went over to see my mother at Winterton, I could not go (as I thought) unless I had had a stiff drink before I went.

So time went by; in some ways the best time of our lives, I suppose, although it is true that every day I spend with Sylvia – certainly every season of the year as it passes, I think has been in most ways the best time of our lives. But Frankfort was in all ways right for us; and then we left it.

Sylvia thinks now, as I sometimes do, that we left it because we were involved in a libel action in Dorset which, as we were undoubtedly in the right, we knew we should find costly. But in fact we had become – not tired of Frankfort, but a little unsettled there. It was hard work and the house could not be run by us alone; we had to have

151

a servant in it. We had a pleasant girl, whom most of the time we liked, but she was very young and we were tied to the place while she was there. And the garden work was too hard for us, and there were outdoor chores, like the hand-pump which was our only means of getting water, which – if ever we could not afford to employ a man to do them, or a man could not be found to be employed – would have become too much for us. These were small things, but others added to them: a murrain among the cats, for instance, which slew all of them with the exception of one breeding female; the fact that my mother lived close enough for there to be little excuse not to visit her and yet the visits took up time that we could ill spare; and (to me especially) an increasing restiveness which I tried to believe was only a yearning for a more simple life, a cottage life again, but which was really the renewal of desperation – desperation because I had found myself incapable of breaking this frightful habit of drinking, and once again I felt that my only hope lay in a drastic change of place and of circumstance. We had visited Chaldon, staying in our own cottage where we had an American friend lodging, who had made it grossly spick-and-span and embellished it with various dreadful improvements. While we were there I had noticed that a larger cottage, towards West Chaldon, was standing empty. This house was near T. F. Powys's and stood on the side of the hill called High Chaldon. There, I thought, right out on the bare side of the hill, it will be difficult to get drink: it will be solitary and sombre and stern and perhaps I shall be able to take myself in hand –

I did not think on, from or to either side, of that impulse: but I obeyed it; and Sylvia – as she has always done all through my most blessed life with her – fell in with my desire so easily and naturally that it was as though the impulse had sprung up in her own heart, and was her own will.

I remember that on the day she had gone to talk to the farmer about letting us this cottage, I was at Beth Car with the American and T. F. Powys and Violet and the child; I could scarcely endure to wait to hear whether they would let us have the place – I felt feverish with anxiety about it; I really did believe, yet again, that my salvation hung on it.

And then Sylvia came in and said that probably we should get it –

We did; and moved there not much later on. My last look at Frankfort, as we drove off in the M.G. car, a little green car which I loved most deeply, with the cat in a hamper, the cat yelling furiously (and he yelled for more than 300 miles almost without a break) and ourselves squeezed up among the luggage; my last look at Frankfort was, alas, a look of shame: deserting that lovely, lovely house because – as I knew beyond any power to evade it – I was rotten and almost destroyed and could not heal myself, even when I was housed in that gentle, beautiful place and had the truest love that ever drew breath in the world. I shall never forget how I felt as I drove the car out of the gate for the last time. I dream of it now, too often, and when I am dead for sure my ghost will haunt there, loving and grieving – there, and along the Drove at Chaldon, where my Love stood beside the thorn tree and vowed her troth to me. Because of that vow and because of our life together I do not think that she will leave me alone, even when I am a ghost; and if she will walk with me, we will be happy – as we always have been, even in despair, together.

I write this on a day when I have heard that at any time

now another one I love will come to live with me here, in this house where Sylvia and I have lived for twelve years together, through bitterness of private woe, through war, through my degradation and shame and through the almost two years accomplished of my heavenly rescue and our increasing happiness and peace. I do not know how this new thing has come about, nor whether it is the work of heaven or hell. I cannot, for more than a moment at a time, realize what it will be like to be here without Sylvia – or anywhere without Sylvia. But I have a conviction that this must be tried; although it is so dangerous that I can scarcely dare measure it even in my fancy.

Whether I have been set askew in my judgement by those long years of drunkenness and waging a useless warfare, I do not know; or whether I am as I feel myself to be: so made that I really can, in truth, be in love with two separate and most alien people. But I know beyond any doubt that my whole being is rooted in Sylvia – that out of my being, however base and bad it seems to be, this matchless love and faith has grown, which is the love she has for me and I have for her. As I write this she is downstairs, listening to some poems of Ronsard being sung on the Third Programme: the sounds come up to me very clearly, and the July evening is slowly darkening. It is just ten o'clock. I know that I shall remember this evening always, and that it may be the most searing torment to my soul, or it may be an almost sweet, light pain, only – remembered when there is no more threat of pain to come.

To this moment, then, my life has been strange and as I have set it down here it has seemed to be unhappy. But in fact it has been one of the most blessed, one of the happiest lives ever lived on the earth: and that fills me with awe and sometimes with trouble, because with far more reason than Nicholas Herman I feel 'That he expected after the pleasant days God had given him he should have his turn of pain and suffering.'

I have had very great suffering and very sharp pain, and bitter shame and grief too, and base and terrible fear; and I cannot think that I have ever *done* anything of myself to be worthy of the least of my joys – and I cannot think that anything in me has deserved one fraction of the love I have had from ordinary people – much less the love Sylvia has given me (but that no one could conceivably 'deserve'; nor is it that quality of love – there is an implication of buying and selling about that word 'deserve', and such love from such as she could not be bought even by God Himself; nor is it of that nature: it is of the nature of something God does – it flows, or it flowers).

Nicholas Herman wrote those words in all simplicity, after he had been into the pit himself, and endured there for four long years 'during which time he suffered much'.

But there is no similarity: 'When I thought of nothing but to end my days in these troubles (which did not at all diminish the trust I had in God, and which served only to increase my faith) ... '

I, too, 'thought of nothing but to end my days in these troubles' – but I had no consciousness of trust in God. Most often, indeed, I had no consciousness at all. But that is untrue. I had all the time two things I believed in: all my life until now I believed in my power to write poetry (I still believe it now, I think, but only as a difficult act of will and faith) and ever since October 1930 I have believed in the truth of our love, Sylvia's and mine. And there has been another thing, but so tenuous and so elusive that I do not know how to describe it: I have *known* God. It is hard to tell how this can be true, and yet I think it is; but I cannot say anything more about it, for that is all I know of it.

There is little more to say; many more things happened, of course. We lived at West Chaldon for several years; made new friends; became interested in politics; travelled in France and went to Spain; and then rented this house, between one visit to Spain and another; and returned here from a holiday in France in 1938, to go through the disgraceful Munich Crisis, and on to the war itself. Between Munich and the war we went to America: Sylvia and I, and E., with whom I had by then fallen in love. Over there everything became chaotic and, for my part, disgraceful. If Sylvia had not stayed by me then I should have been damned out and out. I was lecherous and greedy and drunken there, and yet I had two very serious loves in my heart, even then – and poems, too, in my head.

From 1939 (in October, when Sylvia and I returned to England) until June 1940 we stayed here, and then we went to Norfolk to stay with my mother, expecting the German invasion of England and thinking we should be with her in case we might help her in that time. Many things happened just then, to me, and I drank more, perhaps, than I ever did in my life, until the last year of drinking. I was utterly debased, cowardly, miserable and fraudulent: bringing out remnants of goodness and honour and asserting them as if they were still mine.

We returned here, and I worked in various offices during the war. I was a coward all the time, and even allowed, even asked Sylvia to beg me off from things I dared not face. And she did that for me too. And all the time I was wretchedly going from day to day, week to week, month to month, drinking and trying not to drink; succeeding and falling back again; getting sharper and

156

sharper attacks of unidentified illness, all of which must have been caused by drink or by the strain and shame of my condition. And then the war ended, and still I did not manage to stop.

Until that strange 'crisis' I wrote about at the beginning of this account. And here I am. Whatever happens now, I know that as far as I am concerned everything I have done from that moment, and everything I shall do wrong to my life's end, is of the nature of the one sin that is unforgivable – the sin against the Holy Ghost. And yet I have more hope than fear; more peace than trouble, in the inside of my mind. I do not know why: it could be an infatuated, idiotic optimism; but I think it is what Julian of Norwich says, in a passage Sylvia found for me, when I was saying, being ignorant of her works, that she was an ecstatic, and I had no use for such; so Sylvia opened the book and read it for a moment and then handed it to me, and I read what she pointed out: 'But our good Lord, the Holy Ghost, which is endless life dwelling in our soul, full securely keepeth us; and worketh therein a peace and bringeth it to ease by grace, and accordeth it to God and maketh it pliant. And this is the mercy and the way that our Lord continually leadeth us in as long as we be here in this life which is changeable ... '

Other books from Methuen Paperbacks

BIOGRAPHY

Philippe Julian and John Phillips
VIOLET TREFUSIS: A BIOGRAPHY

Margot Asquith
AN AUTOBIOGRAPHY

POETRY

Brian Gardner (editor)
UP THE LINE TO DEATH
The War Poets 1914–18

Michèle Roberts
MIRROR OF THE MOTHER

Ntozake Shange
FOR COLOURED GIRLS WHO HAVE
CONSIDERED SUICIDE/WHEN THE RAINBOW IS ENUF
A DAUGHTER's GEOGRAPHY

FICTION

Barbara Comyns
THE JUNIPER TREE

Maureen Duffy
GOR SAGA
LONDONERS
WOUNDS
CAPITAL